Praise for
*Journalists and Their Shadows*

"Patrick Lawrence, as witty and cunning as they come, has written both a rapturous and knife-wielding history of journalism in the post-WWII days of America's containment. His love for our flawed profession and his delight in having been in the mix of it makes his regrets and criticisms ring with only the best of intentions. It also is a hell of a lot of fun to read."

—SEYMOUR HERSH

"Patrick Lawrence has written an outstanding, eloquent book about journalism. It is angry and bracing and wise, and it gives us hope. It says the subversion of much of our craft to raw propaganda is not yet complete and a 'Fifth Estate' of independent truth-tellers is rising. One truth is enduring: that we journalists are nothing if not servants of people, never of power."

—JOHN PILGER

"This richly evocative book masquerades as the memoir of a globe-trotting foreign correspondent. At heart it is much more: the poignant story of how an idealistic reporter watched his beloved profession collapse. This is a vivid account of how American journalism degenerated into public relations, what effect that has had on our democracy, and what we can do about it."

—STEPHEN KINZER

"Today, American mainstream journalism has lost all credibility due to its role as an agent of power. From a long personal effort to see and tell the truth in both mainstream and independent news outlets, Patrick Lawrence makes an eloquent plea for the revival of honest journalism able to bring Americans into the diverse world of the 21st century, a world of understanding and mutual respect rather than arrogant attempts to assert U.S. will. His hope lies in the determination of journalists themselves to assert their own inner integrity, to find their true selves by devotion to the truth."

—DIANA JOHNSTONE

## Praise continued:

"A vital, timely book to understand what's long been wrong with establishment media, which has grown far worse since 9/11. Reporters live vicariously through the powerful people they cover, failing to grasp the greater power they hold to cut the powerful to size. Corporate journalists promote a U.S. foreign policy agenda rather than portraying the drama of international conflict with no dog in the fight. Having worked in mainstream journalism as Patrick Lawrence, and having experienced the divided-self he so well describes in these pages, his work resonates with reporters who've taken refuge in independent media. Would that more corporate reporters, pushed by the independents, have the conscience to understand Lawrence and free themselves, and the public."

—JOE LAURIA

"For anyone who takes seriously the Jeffersonian assertion that a free press is the essential condition of a government of the free, this quite brilliant and thankfully pithy alarm bell of a book by veteran foreign correspondent Patrick Lawrence is an indispensable read. A joy to read by a master of the craft of literary journalism honed over decades writing for the sophisticated audience of the *International Herald Tribune* and others who took the fate of the world seriously. Lawrence is surprisingly optimistic about the prospect for a new generation of working-stiff journalists to salvage this indispensable craft despite or because of the wild wired world of the internet."

—ROBERT SCHEER

"Patrick Lawrence draws from a lifetime of hard-won experience and wisdom to chronicle, eulogize, and resurrect the spirit of an American journalism dedicated to the truth. *Journalists and Their Shadows* is a sober and heartening read in these cataclysmic times!"

—AARON GOOD

"Patrick Lawrence's cri de coeur leaps out of decades of variegated—often painful—personal experience in the trenches. He confronts his Jungian 'shadow' with disarming honesty and challenges fellow journalists to integrate their own into an 'undivided self' able to resist pressure to conform. Gentle with the scalpel, Lawrence points to hopeful signs that integrity may one day rescue the profession."

—RAY MCGOVERN

# Journalists and Their Shadows

## Patrick Lawrence

Clarity Press, Inc.

ISBN: 978-1-949762-78-5
EBOOK ISBN: 978-1-949762-79-2

In-house editor: Diana G. Collier
Book design: Becky Luening

Cover photo: Detail, "News," sculpture by Isamu Noguchi at
Rockefeller Center Plaza, Manhattan, New York City. Source:
Wikimedia Commons

Certain passages in this book have appeared, sometimes in very
different form, in the *International Herald Tribune,* the *Far Eastern
Economic Review,* the *National Guardian, The Washington Quarterly,
Bloomberg News, Salon, CounterPunch, The Nation, Raritan,
Consortium News, ScheerPost, Current Concerns, Horizons et débats,*
and *Zeit–Fragen.*

Library of Congress Control Number: 2023934016

Clarity Press, Inc.
2625 Piedmont Rd. NE, Ste. 56
Atlanta, GA 30324, USA
https://www.claritypress.com

This book is for Sheila and Chalmers Johnson, *i.m.*

*During the journey we commonly forget its goal. Almost every profession is chosen and commenced as a means to an end but continued as an end in itself. Forgetting our objectives is the most frequent of all acts of stupidity.*

——Nietzsche,
*The Wanderer and His Shadow,*
1880.

# Contents.

# Introduction.

WHEN WE LOOK BACK NOW on the excesses of the Cold War decades—those few of us inclined to look back—it is commonly with some combination of contempt and derision. Or we simply marvel, without wondering why, at the spectacle of a nation tipped inexplicably into a terrible foolishness. Joe McCarthy's anti-Communist inquisitions, the fallout shelters and civil-defense drills, the loyalty oaths and compulsive patriotism, the blacklists: We presume the wisdom of the decades as we consider those intemperate times: The past was evil, but the evil has passed; they did things differently back then.

I lived through the Cold War but for its very first years, and my memories remain vivid. It is the hysteria in the press and over the broadcast waves that lingers most in my mind. These things have left scars that do not fade with time, and in this I cannot be alone. This hysteria was at its highest pitch during the nineteen fifties and some of the sixties. The major dailies and the networks gave that time its texture and timbre. They delivered the Cold War to our doorsteps, to our car radios, into our living rooms. They defined a consciousness. They told Americans who they were and what made them American and altogether what made America America. A free press was fundamental to this self-image, and Americans nursed a deep need to believe they had one. Our newspapers and networks went to elaborate lengths to give this appearance of freedom and independence. That this was a deception—that American media had surrendered themselves to the new national security state and its various Cold War crusades—is now an open-and-shut matter of record. I count it among the bitterest truths of last seventy-five years of American history.

I do not think, and haven't for a long time thought, that we have any ground to recall our media's Cold War derelictions from a position of distanced superiority. Our press and broadcasters are again in crisis,

1

and it is startling to find how faithfully they repeat the lapses and betrayals of those earlier decades. From Jefferson's day to ours it has been well understood that a democratic polity requires an informed public, and an informed public requires a vital and genuinely free press. We have such a press no more now than we had one during the worst of the Cold War years. Many Americans, still possessed of the need to believe they have a free press that serves them with integrity, are unaware of this crisis. They know nothing of it. I take this—to me a strange, insistent naïveté—as one measure of the urgency of our circumstances, of the dark that has again descended.

The crisis I will address in these pages belongs to all of us, then—to journalists, certainly, but also to the readers and viewers who look to them for reliable, disinterested accounts of our world as it is. We are all in trouble, and it is essential to understand that our trouble has a history if we are to find our way out of it. This is my starting point as I begin these chapters. My finishing point, if I can put it this way, is that there is a path forward from what we should recognize as the extremity of our predicament.

Most Americans, I will say with confidence and dismay all at once, do not know of a way forward from our media's betrayals any more than they know these media have betrayed them. Alas, this, too, is just as it was during the Cold War. But the emergence of genuinely independent media—independent media as against mainstream media, or legacy media, or corporate-owned media—seems to me to hold a promise that flickered but never flamed when the Cold War defined who Americans were and what they thought. In independent publications and the journalists who staff them I find the prospect of renewal—of reinvention, even—of a kind few of us could have imagined even a couple of decades ago. Their work stands to spare us the indignity of repeating past errors in a perverse, endless loop. I see in it, and in those who read it, listen to it, or watch it, a shared determination to do better, a shared longing for true accountings of events. Doing better requires that we transcend the ways our traditional media organize themselves and operate.

These may seem idle thoughts, or wishful thinking, or a case of undue optimism, accustomed as many of us are to assuming our major dailies and broadcast networks remain impeccable sources of factual accuracy. I turn to Bergson and how he understood the coming of great change when such uncertainties come upon me:

> It is a leap forward, which can take place only if a society has decided to try the experiment; and the experiment will not be tried unless a society has allowed itself to be won over, or at least stirred.... It is no use maintaining that this leap forward does not imply a creative effort behind it... That would be to forget that most great reforms appeared at first impracticable, as in fact they were.

Such is my reply to the charge of *angélisme,* as the French say—of otherworldly idealism. To me, it is among independent journalists and their publications that we find the profession's dynamism—its vitality, its return to itself as an independent pole of power. And I detect among Americans a gathering readiness to make the leap these publications will require and enable. Pessimists as to our press's performance and prospects are many and their justifications plentiful. I, writing after many years in the mainstream press and nearly as many with a hand in one or another independent publication, am not among them.

I HAVE NEVER BEEN MUCH for golden ages, and certainly I've never lived through one. For a time during the mid–Cold War years many journalists imagined that they had begun to restore the craft to a lost integrity after the compromises of the nineteen forties, fifties, and sixties. There was the best of the Vietnam coverage, publication of the Pentagon Papers, the breaking of the Watergate scandal. A little off to the side there was a lively "alternative" press. The thought arose among journalists at the big dailies and the major broadcasters that news media could be transformed from within by those who populated their newsrooms. A golden age, no. But an optimism of this kind was in the very air I breathed as I set out to make myself a journalist.

There was a place in the mainstream then, if not a large place, for journalists who held to the ideals, principles, and purpose that commonly draw people into the profession. But this place began to close when the 1975 defeats in Southeast Asia so severely wounded the American psyche and rattled the power elite. Then it disappeared, more or less completely, as the Cold War years gave way to the post–Cold War triumphalism that marked the nineteen nineties. There followed the events of 2001. These proved a decisive moment in our media's return to the worst of the many bad habits they had formed during the nineteen fifties.

America assumed a defensive crouch after the 11 September attacks in New York and Washington, the belligerent crouch of the wounded and uncertain. Its leaders seemed to turn away from the world and against it all at once. They were no longer interested in how events might look to other eyes: The American perspective was the only perspective that mattered. The press and broadcasters reflected this blustery jingoism as they once again enlisted themselves and their readers and viewers in the national security state's cause. Their purpose turned, subtly at first and then very plainly, from informing the public to protecting the institutions they purported to report upon from the public's gaze.

Fifteen years after the 2001 events came the fiasco we named "Russiagate." I will have much to say in these pages about this heatedly contested episode. For now, this: Russiagate worsened what was, by 2016, a crisis not only in our media but in our polity. An unthinking allegiance to authority has taken root—this in paradoxical response, so far as I can tell, to the increasing incoherence of our institutions, of our idea of ourselves and our place in the world, of our national life altogether. The conduct of the press has proven pivotal in bringing Americans to this woeful state.

Would there have been a Cold War if the American press hadn't promoted it as assiduously as it did? At the very least it is an interesting question. Would we find ourselves today in a second Cold War—and a hot war by proxy in Ukraine—had our media not insisted for five years, with the flimsiest evidence and most often none, that Russia had somehow corrupted our elections to gain control of the White House? This seems to me too obvious to merit debate.

Is the condition of our press now less extreme than it was during the Cold War, is it roughly comparable, or is it worse? I have considered this question many times since 2001, by myself and with others. I tilt to the last of these possibilities. We now live with a regime of censorship made all the more perverse by the enthusiastic support of many journalists working for corporate newspapers and networks.

The major dailies and the wire services routinely report the assertions of government officials as if these assertions alone were evidence of their veracity. Television broadcasters feature former intelligence operatives and military officers as impartial news analysts. I mark a lot of this down to the paranoia, so redolent of the nineteen fifties, that our media fostered during the Russiagate frenzy. The crisis in Ukraine has amplified this—worsening what a lot of us thought could not get any worse.

At this point who can see an end to the degeneration of our media and our public discourse? Each spurs the other to new levels of degradation and incoherence. Those committed to defending the First Amendment are dismissed as "free speech absolutists." We are now treated to purportedly responsible commentators calling for the arrest and trial, on charges of treason, of those who depart from the xenophobic orthodoxy on any question to do with Russia. As I wrote these pages the Department of Homeland Security announced it had formed a Disinformation Governance Board to identify what it deems mis- and disinformation "threats" from Russian media reports and reports from anywhere that "undermine public trust in our democratic institutions." No major daily or network broadcaster published a critique of the new DHS agency when the department disclosed—after the fact—it had launched it.

It was difficult to refute the common charge that this was anything other than a Ministry of Truth straight out of Orwell, and the DHS project was subsequently "paused" in apparent response to the outrage it prompted. But the department's plan was merely one especially egregious manifestation of what we now call "the disinformation industry." The major social media platforms are committed participants in this malign enterprise. It also consists of self-appointed groups, typically staffed and advised by former intelligence and law-enforcement operatives, that serve as privatized versions of the short-lived governance board. Though purporting to expose agents of Russian propaganda and disinformation, in truth their intent is to discredit or otherwise suppress dissent. The record of those whose reputations these groups have attacked—mine among them—makes this perfectly clear.

How much daylight is left between our traditional media and the powers they are charged to report upon? I see next to none. Propaganda carries a whiff of the foreign for most Americans, who take it to be an affliction common to corrupt or despotic societies far removed from ours. But I am not alone when I assert that American media have come to serve the purposes of official propagandists. To find this thought shocking or hyperbolic is to admit ignorance of the history I consider it essential for us to grasp. The press and broadcasters as we have them are simply putting back on the fashions they wore during those decades we like to think are well behind us.

The Ukraine crisis, as it erupted into open conflict in early 2022, has made various of these stark realities plain. Our major media uncritically reproduce what government agencies—the State Department, the Department of Defense—publicly acknowledge is propaganda in the cause of an "information war," rendering this, so far as I know, the first conflict in modern history with no objective coverage in our mainstream media of day-to-day events and their context. I have mentioned the need common among Americans to believe a principled, independent press serves them. This need deepened after the events of September 2001—one consequence of the psychological disorientation that has followed from that time. And it deepens still. However distressing we may find our media's malpractice as it covers the Ukraine conflict, the public's acquiescence in their ignorance of events is equally concerning. Tell us what to think and believe, many Americans seem to say, and we will think and believe it. Show us some pictures, for images are all.

THERE WAS NO SUCH THING as digital media during the Cold War, of course. There was an independent press, but its reach was limited and its resources yet more so. The big dailies, *The New York Times* in the lead, were content to ignore it. In my early years at independent newspapers and magazines we accepted this as a given and got on with the work, however few our readers and however short the money. The prevalence of digital media now has changed more or less everything. The independent media I will write of—lively, un-shy in their explorations, gaining in influence—would not be possible were it not for the publishing platforms digital technologies open to them.

But as so often, with success come liabilities. It is the increasing visibility and impact of these media that in large measure prompt the plague of censorship that now besets us.

Since the Russiagate uproar, social media have become the field of battle on which the corporate press and the technology monopolies—the latter under incessant pressure from Capitol Hill—wage war for "control of the narrative." This is a combative fight mainstream media never before had to take up, for they have never heretofore had to defend their monopoly on information in the public sphere. To describe it as fierce is to put the point too mildly. Many livelihoods and reputations have already been lost to it. Independent journalists, I among them, are routinely "canceled," or "de-platformed"—banished, in plain English—from social media. The work of independent practitioners, often years of it, can be removed from public view in a matter of minutes. Once again, we must be mindful of Cold War antecedents as this antidemocratic spectacle unfolds in the name of democracy and a defense against what is so cavalierly labeled "disinformation." This, as I have just suggested, comes very close to meaning the elimination of all dissenting perspectives.

This commotion does not surprise me. If changes of any magnitude and consequence will seem at first impractical, neither do they come easily. What is entrenched and vested is bound to resist what obliges it to do things differently. This is our circumstance. This is what we see if we are paying attention, a contention between what is old and what proposes to be. The warfare we witness can be taken in this way as an advance, a measure of movement in a new direction.

It is early days yet. The first independent publications to make use of digital technologies appeared in the mid-nineteen nineties, and for a long time there were few of them. But they are destined to assume an ever-larger role in the way Americans inform themselves. While it is highly unlikely at this point, we must hold out the possibility that the work of dedicated independent publications will eventually inspire (or require) the corporate press and broadcasters to restore to themselves what they long ago surrendered.

The best independent media already bring to light significant and cogently reported stories mainstream media misreport or leave unreported. To consider this thought in its broadest sense: Independent journalists have it within them to help bring critical thinking back into our discourse, to cultivate the habits of discernment, autonomous judgment, and, not at all least, to make possible a new, true accounting of ourselves—a new narrative that I am convinced most of us are eager to have and live by.

Am I suggesting we stand at the eve of a golden age at last? No, again. Independent publications have a lot of growing to do, a lot of maturing. There is weeding to be done in the garden. There is experience to be accumulated, there are mistakes to be made and learned from, there are resources to be marshaled, there are reputations to be built, egos to be tamed, and amateurs to fall by the wayside. But I see in independent media the promise of reinvigoration. Implicit in the best of their work is a revived understanding of the journalist's proper location between readers and viewers on one hand and, on the other, the powers he or she reports upon. Power: In a single phrase, the journalist's relationship to power is the subject of this book. In independent media I see a chance for the profession to reconstitute itself by reclaiming the power that is its alone.

I WAS AMONG THOSE young hopefuls when, in the early nineteen seventies, I determined to make journalism my profession. But my faith in what could be done in corporate newspapers was attenuated from the first. At twenty-two I was well aware of what the press had made of itself since the Cold War's onset in the late nineteen forties—its compromises with power, its service as an appendage of the national security state. I seem to have understood from my earliest years—and I am not sure how or why, given my inexperience—that the true future of journalism (or the future of true journalism) lay not so much in independent editors, reporters, or correspondents surviving at this or that newspaper, but in independent journalism altogether.

I soon found work at a publication dedicated to this latter thought. But it was difficult then, if not impossible, to sustain oneself as an independent journalist. This was a matter of poor pay only in part. I also found the professional standards very low. People were not trained in the disciplines of the craft. This showed in what we were publishing. My professional life, in consequence, was divided for many years, a little in the way of Stevenson's Jekyll and Hyde. From corporate newspapers and newsmagazines, I learned a respect for technical excellence—the how-to of the craft. I still consider this essential to the credibility of the work. From the independent publications where I wrote or edited, for a long time in a moonlighting capacity, I learned that principles and ethical standards must be held beyond negotiation, that they often had a price attached to them, and that one had to be willing to pay this price to get consistently good work done. Defining my professional life for some years in this peculiar way was a necessity, and I accepted it as such.

After nearly a decade as an editor in New York, I resigned from *The New York Times* and went abroad to begin many more years as a correspondent, chiefly but not only in Asia. Three of the publications that employed me were generous with the freedom they afforded those who staffed them. Maybe it was for this reason I naturally gravitated toward the *Far Eastern Economic Review, The Christian Science Monitor,* and the *International Herald Tribune.* These were among the weeklies and dailies that had kept open those small places I mentioned earlier, wherein independent journalists could do their work without bending to ideological pretense or surrendering their principles. All three were written and edited from a perspective more worldly than national, a distinction that came to matter greatly to me. Alas, two of these three are now no more, early casualties of the crisis to come; *The Monitor* soldiers on as best it can.

The work I did for independent publications over many years, sometimes writing under pen names or without bylines, mattered as much to me as anything else I did, if not more. But for a long time, this was the work of a shadow self. Here I borrow from Jung, who seems to have borrowed from Nietzsche. Each of us has a shadow, the Swiss psychoanalyst explained here and there in many of his works. It is that part of ourselves that is suppressed by convention, orthodox morality, acceptable taste, the exactions of employers, and other forms of social and professional intimidation. The casualty of these infinitely manifest forces is the integrated personality—the authentic, undivided self, capable of judging and acting with certainty and without reference to the coercions of power or collective opinion.

The shadow selves of journalists should be of special concern to all of us. They have been among my abiding preoccupations, certainly, since my years in the mainstream press. It is when journalists divide their personalities to secure and hold positions in corporate media, as is all too common, that judgments are compromised and the corruptions and delinquencies that beset the profession begin. When I write of my shadow, I mean that part of myself that I kept hidden from others. For a long time, I tended to hide it even from myself—if I did not, indeed, hide from it. I earned my living at mainstream newspapers and newsmagazines because that is where you could earn a living during the years of which I write. My work for independent publications—in this private way, a way there was no need for others to see—amounted to my defense against the extinction of my individuality, of who I truly was.

Over time it became evident that the small places I had found in mainstream publications were on the way to disappearing entirely. In the years after the events of 2001, I began to realize a moment of truth, if I can call it this, was coming. At some point it would no longer be possible to do conscionable work in the corporate press.

My moment arrived, a little belatedly it seems to me now, while I was still working abroad. This was in 2006 and 2007, as the wars in Afghanistan and Iraq ground on—the press coverage of which looked to me more boldly dishonest than any I could recall. I had been overseas for nearly three decades. Everything in journalism had begun to change after 2001. Long-frayed standards and ethics were shredded. Facts and logic no longer mattered: These were marshaled merely to serve desired conclusions and secure the public's acquiescence to the policies of the national security state. There was a closure, a shutting down—in newsrooms, in minds—that I could hardly miss. It became clear to me that my years in the mainstream were drawing to a close.

My mind returned to memories of the nineteen fifties and sixties as soon as I arrived home from those years abroad. It was with the Russiagate upheaval some years later that my alternatives finally ran out. I was writing foreign affairs commentary at *The Nation* by then, and I was censored and subsequently fired for refusing to reproduce the official Russophobia in the columns. Holding to all I understood my profession to be would make me an outcast of a sort, a wanderer. And as I embraced my shadow at last, so I became.

M Y PROFESSIONAL HOME for some years has been *Consortium News*. One of the first independent journals to appear on the internet, it was founded in 1995 by the late Robert Parry, a celebrated Associated Press reporter who also sought a refuge from the mainstream and had built his own asylum. *Consortium's* circulation is small but growing, the common state of things at publications of its kind. My work also appears in *ScheerPost,* a publication started by Robert Scheer, among the bright lights in independent journalism since the mid-nineteen sixties. Scheer, along with Warren Hinckle, made *Ramparts* one of the memorable voices of its time. *Consortium* and *ScheerPost* are havens now for reporters, correspondents, and columnists who bring their professional, intellectual, and ethical standards with them when their alternatives in the mainstream, like Bob Parry's and like mine, have run out.

I count myself fortunate to write these pages from the perspective of an independent practitioner. My medium is part of my message, if I can put it this way. I came early to independent journalism, as I will recount in these pages, and now, from here, the possibilities of renewal in the profession are easily evident to me. From here I find, indeed, cause for considerable optimism, strange as this may at first seem to those who see only the dead end of a craft that has drifted so far from what it should be.

"Luck is the residue of design," as one of my *Herald Tribune* editors once told me over the telephone from Paris to Hong Kong. The years I spent contributing to independent publications when there were few of them have served me well in this way since I left corporate newspapers behind. It was my luck to live those years. They showed me the worth and importance of work as an independent journalist no matter what the conditions. They showed me that sacrifices would have to be made but that I could make them with equanimity in the knowledge that I was not betraying myself and that, succeeding in this, I was contributing to the betterment of the profession. Those years kept my shadow alive such that I could one day embrace it, become at one with it.

I have as much time for self-indulgent memoirs as I do for golden ages. In looking back on my decades as a professional, I have sought to bring the past of the Cold War to bear on our present on the thought that it is with this history that we—we, all of us—will be able to think through our present predicaments with clarity instead of conformity to coercive frames of thought. In sharing a little of my story I wish to

suggest what is possible, what all journalists have it within themselves
to do if they set their minds to it. I offer my own experience to demonstrate that, with effort and determination, there is an alternative to the
alienation the profession imposes on journalists—to "dis-integration,"
to the loss of touch with our shadow selves. The future of my profession, it is not too much to say, will be shaped decisively by what every
journalist does in the matter of his or her shadow.

There is the question of language, a recurring topic in these
pages. We can use it differently. It can be our curative. With clear,
plain language we can reconnect ourselves with reality rather than, as
it is so often now, using it to render us and the public for whom we
write separate, uncomprehending, distant, alienated from the world as
it is.

There is the matter of how we live. For journalists to resituate
themselves in relation to the powers they report upon means to relo-
cate themselves in society—a question of status and class. It is time
for journalists to set aside their pretenses, nursed for a century now
in the name of "professionalism," that they are among the elites they
are charged to report on and write about. This distracting aspiration
has done nothing but damage since it arose by way of figures such as
Walter Lippmann in the nineteen twenties. It leaves journalists now
in the wrong place. I propose a going back, a return to what it used
to mean to be a journalist. I call this "a poor journalism," by which I
mean an authentic journalism, a journalism stripped to its essentials,
a craft infinitely richer than what we have now. I could not have said
any of these things were I standing anywhere other than where I am.

Many years before I trained myself to be a journalist, I stood
one spring afternoon before a painting in a Paris museum. It was a
Delaunay from 1912, filled with luminous color and lyrical lines in
the style called Orphism. I was twenty and just learning to look at
paintings. I remember, even now, the freedom and kinetic energy in it,
the never-before-done of it. An intuition unmediated by thought came
to me, something I all at once knew. Artists produce enduring can-
vases, work that changes the way we see, when they must. If Robert
Delaunay didn't have to paint *La Ville de Paris,* he wouldn't have. And
this is how it often is, I suddenly saw, for anyone doing original work,
work that advances the human cause. So frequently there is no choice,

it is the only way forward; the available alternatives are convention and empty repetition.

For many years after that afternoon in Paris I wondered if I would ever find myself with my back to the wall as I imagined Delaunay had when he was twenty-six or twenty-seven. There would be burdens: Living and working on one's own terms always comes with these. I didn't wonder about that. I wondered whether I would understand burdens as blessings and whether I would be wise enough to make the most of any that might come to me. It is part of my luck, too, that my back was, after many years, so situated: It was then, finally, I was able fully to inhabit what I am calling my shadow.

I am certain my profession is heavily populated with reporters, editors, and correspondents with shadows very like mine. If each of us has a shadow, and the struggle is to keep our relations with our shadows alive, this is especially important in the case of journalists, given the profound consequences it has for how journalists do their work and for every reader and viewer who looks to them. Journalism as we now have it requires those practicing it to accept a pernicious division within themselves. There is the self as presented and performing, and the reintegrated self, and it is the performer that insistently demands precedence. In my view—and my view derives from my experience and what I have observed in others—independent media are sites where the journalist can refuse what amounts to a required "dis-integration" in favor of a recovered wholeness in the personality and the work. This is another reason I count these media important.

This divided self is another subject I mean to explore in these pages. It is a psychological question for the journalist in our time, a psychosocial question that is unexamined but of great importance. The local pastor in my small New England town taught me the intimate relationship between "integration" and "integrity"—a connection right before my eyes but one I had never seen. In his excellent spirit, what I have to say is an argument for reintegration—a reclamation of integrity. I hope those journalists who have begun to question the unethical compromises work in corporate media requires can understand the matter this way. These pages are for everyone, but they are meant especially for them—the refugees and those who, starting out on independent publications, have not had to accept their own "dis-integration."

I began this book as an essay intended to appear in *Raritan*, the quarterly journal, and it has since grown well beyond its original bounds. These pages are an act of retrieval, as all true writing is so far as I am concerned. My intent is to redeem dignity from what has descended into lamentable ignominy. Even the weak and destructive propel us, providing we are able to discern what they have done and go on to transcend it.

# 1.

# 'What Men Wished to See.'

> And the symbols most effective in
> the formation of public opinion are
> those most remote from reality.
>
> ——Jacques Ellul,
> *Propaganda,*
> 1962.

THE IMMENSE GOSS PRESSES on the third floor sounded like distant tanks as they rolled in the evenings. You knew they had started by the muffled rumble coursing through the Daily News Building on East Forty-Second Street. In the newsroom, four stories higher, the floor shivered. The bulldog, the first edition of the night, would be on trucks in a matter of minutes, ink still fresh enough to stain your fingers. Even a neophyte could sense, if subliminally, he was in the presence of something possessed of prodigious power. It came to him through his feet.

So it was for me when, many autumns ago, I arrived at the News Building, that Art Deco jewel halfway between Grand Central Terminal and the United Nations Secretariat. The lobby featured an enormous globe with a brass railing around it. An inlaid compass, brass-bordered and marked with all the world's great cities, sprawled across the marble floor. The ceiling, a dome of dark glass with twinkling stars in it, told you this was a place to be in the universe. And at the entrance, the building's *pièce de résistance*: Atop a bas-relief depicting men and women at work in a busy city, these words: "He made so many of them." The first half of this quotation is left to the inference of those familiar with the famous *mot*, often but erroneously attributed to Lincoln: "God must have loved the common man."

For a child of the sixties not long out of university, becoming staff at *The News* was to labor on the very wrongest side of the divide that even then tormented Americans. The national unity that the Depression and World War II had imparted—"the inner coherence," as Arthur Miller later described it—had begun to fray within a few years of the 1945 victories. A social conscience once shared among Americans, along with the honorable internationalism F.D.R. articulated as the war drew to a close, gave way to a militant xenophobia and "a rising wave of yahooism"—Miller again. By the early nineteen seventies, the Vietnam War had widened and deepened fault lines long earlier manifest as a feature of the American scene.

The *Daily News* as it was in 1973 relished the animus. It was a bullhorn for the love-it-or-leave-it crowd—hyper-patriotic in the commonly mistaken way, still certain there was a Red under every bed. My favorite description of *The News* belongs to James Aronson, who was shortly to figure considerably in my professional odyssey. "It's an obese, malevolent fishwife," the late and distinguished editor told an interviewer not long before I made my way to the seventh-floor newsroom, "screaming obscenities at more than two million persons a day, exhorting them to go out and kill a Commie for Christ—or even just for fun."

In this way *The News* taught me a truth I wish I never had to learn. This is the truth of alienation. You have to accept a greater or lesser degree of it to survive in our major media. And so it is you learn that you have a shadow, a part of yourself you have obscured and with which your relations will be complex. The ideals that draw many of us to the profession come to seem, in time, as quaint as the sentiments found in Jimmy Stewart movies. There is no resisting this alienation, not from within the corporate-owned mainstream. How a newspaper portrays events is the business of the publisher and his senior editors. Journalists—"laborers in the vineyards," as one of my editors used to call us—write for them, not for readers. Objectivity, held high as the profession's ideal, was long ago made the instrument of discipline used to force journalists to write, like ventriloquists' dummies, in the institutional voices of their newspapers. What is published, how it is written, and where it appears in the paper might be argued over, and often are, but at bottom the journalist has two alternatives. For the sake of a paycheck and a promotion, you cultivate an unhealthy detachment from your published work—and so from your shadow as I am using this term—or you assume the editorial stance of your employer. These are not mutually exclusive. Many are they, in my experience, who are alienated from themselves in this way but, thoroughly unaware of their condition, defend with the convert's conviction their newspapers' positions on politics, economics, foreign affairs, what have you. Holding to your principles—defending the integrated self, this is to say—is a third way at the question, but you learn swiftly this is often a pricey proposition, if, indeed, it is not fatal to your prospects.

By and large what I found as I took up the craft was an immense, collective case of *mauvaise foi*, Sartre's "bad faith," a thought I will explore in pages to come. This is yet truer now than it was during the time of which I write. Those who hold privately to their ethics and standards but compromise them in their work become "professionals"—technicians who take pride mostly in the mastery of method. At the other end of the newsroom, journalists who profess the ideologies of those who pay them turn Descartes on his head: "I think, therefore I am" becomes "I am, therefore I think." For every journalist at every newspaper or network, the question is the same: Who am I in the face of a power vastly larger than I, a power beyond my control, a power that makes buildings shake?

I STARTED AT THE NEWS as a copyboy, an all-but-extinct species now. This meant I was "on the bench," any one of several scattered around the newsroom. One hopped to at the call of "Copy!"—a word I soon learned had limitlessly nuanced intonations. The main chore was bearing stories one take (page) at a time from reporters to editors and from editors to other editors until the final markup disappeared down to the composing room by way of a frayed rubber conveyor belt or an antiquated pneumatic tube. There was also the fetching of files from the morgue, the clipping library, or film from photographers out shooting, or sandwiches, or dry cleaning, or bottles of sherry for the weekend editor. I was occasionally assigned a staff car to take a copy of the bulldog to Suzy Knickerbocker, a.k.a. Aileen Mehle, the glamorous gossip columnist, in her stylish *maisonette* off Fifth somewhere in the East Sixties.

I absorbed like a sponge the "how" of it, the craft. After a time, I followed the conveyor belt down a flight to the composing room, where I learned what it meant to edit "on the stone," when pages were typeset and assembled in metal forms. These were the last years of hot type, the nineteenth-century technology that set lines of text in molten lead. As each edition came into being, the clatter of Linotype operators made the sixth floor sound like a mah-jongg parlor. I still remember how the pace built as press time drew near. Stories had to be shortened by one or two or five lines, or "widows"—short lines—trimmed. Stories had to be "leaded out" if too short—all this within minutes and with no room for botch. A cold mastery was essential down in that gritty, fluorescent-lit sprawl, printers in caps of folded newsprint awaiting an editor's direction.

The composing room, last stop in the editorial process, was a good place to conclude my apprenticeship. Some of what I learned has gone the way of green eyeshades and shirtsleeve garters. Editing on paper required knowledge of a system of symbols that would be hieroglyphics to someone coming to the craft now. No one any longer knows (or needs to) how to edit leaded type. But I wouldn't surrender any of it for the all-around nous that was there for the learning, provided you remained open to a certain osmosis. The *Daily News* was also an excellent place to acquire the habits that made good sentences. The imperatives of tight writing—simplicity, spareness of style—were commandments in the newsroom that required no mention. "Best read because we're best written" was among *The News*'s advertising lines at the time. I can't imagine who recruited Truman Capote to recite it in a television spot, but so he did. The paper deserved the boast.

It was all technique for me, in short. The John Wayne nationalism, the barking paranoia about "Russ"—headline language for the Soviet Union—would have to be set aside for the time being, my acquiescence to alienation. Even then I knew my years at *The News* were worth magnitudes more than what any journalism school—sandboxes, in our rough-and-tumble assessment—could impart in thrice the time. I still think jumping feet first into the flowing stream is the best way to begin in the profession. "With prolonged drowning shall develop gills," as Auden wrote in the early poem he called "The Journey."

One day not long before my last, I fell into a conversation with an editor who had come down to the composing room after the two-star edition was on the presses and there was an exhale before the three-star got going. His name was John Collins, and he had taken to looking out for me in a bemused sort of way. Maybe John knew I was planning my departure, I can't recall. "Don't forget this about newspapers," he said with that Irish smile I still picture clearly. "Get in, get wise, and get out." I understood the bittersweet thought by then. "Journalism will kill you, but it will keep you alive while you're at it"—I had already come across Horace Greeley's adage. It occurs to me all these years later that John was suspended, I'm sure by choice, between the second and third of the imperatives he cited. And I found myself, for a long time and not unhappily, somewhere between the first and second, the third unthought of until many years later, when the profession lapsed into the crisis now evident all around us.

ONE EVENING EARLY in my *Daily News* days, I finished my shift and set out for Costello's, a celebrated writers' bar on Third Avenue in the Forties. Costello's was where I gleaned lessons of another kind, those having to do with the culture of the craft. I had with me a fresh edition of a motley monthly called *[MORE]*. The title alone conveyed an abiding affection for what was by this time a troubled, uncertain profession. "[MORE]" was a little in the way of a secret handshake, a touch exclusionary when used as a magazine title. It was what reporters typed at the foot of a take if additional takes were to come. The last take was marked "—30—" for reasons no one has ever persuasively fathomed. Who outside the profession would know of these things?

*[MORE]* was written by and for self-examining journalists who understood that the craft had grown complacent, encrusted with conventions, ideologically hidebound. A renovation was required—this was the subtext running through *[MORE]*'s tabloid pages. They articulated a subculture, with a whiff of the then-fashionable counterculture in the magazine's first years. It gave a new arrival a way into the thoughtful end of the craft—a window through which to see the educated professionals who staffed the newsrooms at the big dailies and the networks.

Costello's was something different. It was a place where you
might seek that grail misanthropic writers yearn for, and for my money
most true writers are misanthropes: You might find the cup of shared
belonging sitting there on the bar. It had opened as a speakeasy during
the Prohibition years, and a lot of great names had bellied up before
I set foot in the place—A. J. Liebling, John O'Hara, Joseph Mitchell,
a Parnassus of others. Hemingway makes an apparently apocryphal
appearance in the long story. Thurber covered one smoke-stained plas-
ter wall with his celebrated caricatures. Being there was part of a long
rite of passage. I might have been a broken barstool pushed against a
wall for all I mattered to anyone else: I was an eavesdropper listening
to what my profession sounded like.

No one from *[MORE]* would've spent an evening at Costello's.
This was a grittier, plainer-spoken crowd—professional but not "professionalized" as the writers and editors at *[MORE]* were. It had a whiff
of the museum about it by my time. You could taste what remained of
that certain-of-itself world passing not all that gently into the precincts
of memory and nostalgia. I wanted to know this taste, nonetheless. I
wanted to feel, and vicariously would do, the ease and solidity I saw in
the older habitués. Along with their been-there-and-back knowingness
there was a stranded innocence, too, a lingering dream of order, and,
ever faintly, a confusion and anxiety as to a world outside Costello's
worn wooden doors that didn't match theirs. To venture a paradox, I
wanted to know best as I could a world I would never know.

How excellent I must have thought it was to read *[MORE]* while
perched on one of those scarred barstools. If memory serves, on
the evening I recall I was intent on a page-one piece by the late and
inimitable Alexander Cockburn. It was headlined "How to Earn Your
Trench Coat" and was a barbed skewering of the worn-out imagery and
hollow pretensions of the foreign correspondent, in particular those of
*The New York Times*'s C. L. Sulzberger, whose columns accumulated
the profession's clichés like barnacles on a sailboat's bow. This puts
me in May 1974, when Cockburn's piece appeared. With *[MORE]*
spread open before me, the future lay draped atop the past as I read
page to page. I can still taste the Harp I preferred at the time.

The scene I describe puts me in mind of what I learned years later
from D. H. Lawrence, Walter Gropius, and a few others: To add to tradition you must break with tradition. Anything else is sterile imitation.

In time original work, one's departures, become part of the tradition. "True tradition is the result of constant growth," Gropius wrote in, of all places, the *Harvard Alumni Bulletin*. The year was 1950, and the Bauhaus founder stood against the reproduction of buildings in Harvard Gothic style around the Yard. "New buildings must be invented, not copied," he wrote. "The great periods of architecture in the past have never imitated the periods of their forefathers."

I knew nothing of this thought during the days I recount. But somewhere within me was the impulse learn the tradition and then, one way or another, turn against it the way Gropius advocated. I would've done something else before making myself into a mimic. I was an altar boy holding cruets at the *Daily News*; at Costello's I was more or less invisible. Attentive enough in both places, I knew—an intuition—that I belonged to a different order. I nursed the extravagant desire to write of what I thought important, to write it as I meant it, and to write it for readers as against publishers. Even the reform-from-within ethos implicit in most of what *[MORE]* published seemed to me short of what I thought my generation ought to strive for.

What was that?

How achieve it?

My thoughts wandered. Soon enough so did I.

JOURNALISTS WERE FLUSH with confidence during my apprentice years. *The New York Times, The Washington Post,* and *The Boston Globe* had published the Pentagon Papers two years before I walked into the Daily News Building and defended their right to do so before the Supreme Court. This was a radical ripping of the veil off twenty years of official lies, covert operations, and misrepresentations of the war in Indochina. Who could be other than stunned by these revelations and impressed with the press's audacity and determination? "The Fourth Estate" had long earlier taken on the dust of a neglected antique, the notion of another age. But it was possible, with the release of the Pentagon Papers, to think again of the press as the independent pole of power a working democracy needed it to be.

Two summers later the Watergate story began to break open in all its sordid detail. The press again stood in righteous opposition to the government it reported on. Concurrent with these events, a handful of distinguished correspondents in Saigon—prominent among them David Halberstam of *The Times,* Neil Sheehan of United Press International and subsequently *The Times,* and Malcolm Browne of The Associated Press—had reported Vietnam as the defeat-in-the-making it proved to be in 1975. Michael Herr published *Dispatches,* his searingly honest account of Vietnam at ground level, in 1977. This work was another badge of courage on the American press's chest.

Much of the pride and confidence these performances imparted required qualification. I question—I doubt, indeed—whether *The Times, The Post,* and *The Globe* would have published the Pentagon Papers had sentiment in high places not begun to shift against the Indochina war. Most of those filing reports critical of the Vietnam War wrote not out of principled objection to American aggression but because they, along with many in government, had concluded the war could not be won—two different standards of judgment. The Watergate story that propelled Carl Bernstein and Bob Woodward to fame may not have come to light had certain factions of Washington's permanent bureaucracy not wished to depose a president they found objectionable in one or another way.

In hindsight, I think Watergate—and maybe the Pentagon Papers, too—did journalism harm as well as good. In re-legitimating the mainstream, they calmed a gathering wave of criticism within the profession and a longstanding distrust among readers and viewers—both heartily deserved. Intrepid poses have been struck a thousand times since. Watergate gave the newly fashionable investigative journalism an elevated place in newsrooms and the popular imagination alike. Here was an endeavor that would get to the bottom of whatever dark depth needed to be plumbed. Investigative journalism was and is a lot less heroic, in my view. The focus on this or that wrongdoing made reporters look Clark Kent valiant while excusing them from examining the larger circumstances—political, social, economic—that led to the wrongdoing. Causality, in other words, tended to be left out. The Watergate story was attractive in and out of the profession because it was self-contained in the fate of one man and threatened no one with the imperative to consider systemic dysfunctions. Considering the many momentous matters that go uninvestigated, the investigative enterprise often amounts to posturing. *[MORE]*, seduced by Woodward and Bernstein's triumph, succumbed swiftly to this illusion.

*[MORE]* featured all manner of topics in its pages—gender and race in the newsroom, corporate advertising, obscenity and profanity questions. Every issue was an argument for a press free of ideologies and orthodoxies, a press that insisted on its independence. Much happened during *[MORE]*'s eight years of publication, 1971 to 1978. The fence posts defining what was permissible to report and how reporters wrote about it moved outward, if marginally. Whatever the limitations of investigative journalism, the best of it was very good. The "underground press," inspired in part by the antiwar movement and the fantasy of a counterculture, rose and declined but left its mark on the profession.

But some things that ought to have happened did not. Even the most committed press critics failed to address what any journalist worthy of the designation ought to have been railing against by the early nineteen seventies. Banging shoes on desks, Khrushchev-style, would have been perfectly justified. The question had to do with the profession's relations with power, a topic that will never be far in these pages. The press's proximity to power—at this time political and corporate—was considered, as I now reflect, a matter too large and consequential to engage. To understand our moment, we must understand this. Readers and viewers still live with the consequences of this collective flinch. So do our newspapers and broadcasters and all who work for them.

THE AMERICAN PRESS cooperated closely with political and military authorities during World War II. This is what happens in wartime, for better or worse. The question confronting Roosevelt as World War II drew to a close was how swiftly he could dismantle the wartime military machine and its intelligence appendage, the Office of Strategic Services. Had he lived to do so, Roosevelt would have unmade a consciousness, too. But by 1947, F.D.R. two years dead, Truman, his generals, and America's founding Cold Warriors had other plans. Permanent, self-sustaining bureaucracies were in the making. The military machine would remain and grow ever more immense. By a directive long kept secret, Truman authorized the National Security Agency five years later. In all of this, the wartime consciousness was sustained more or less intact. So was the wartime relationship between

the press and the powers it reported upon. The press was not conscripted into the Cold War: It enlisted.

There is some history to consider. American journalism had
already been pressed into service against the Bolsheviks as the events
of 1917 unfolded. Walter Lippmann and Charles Merz, prominent
journalists of the time, anatomized *The New York Times* coverage in
"A Test of the News," an essay published in *The New Republic* in
1920. Their findings made perfectly plain *The Times*'s fidelity to the
Wilson administration's interests as these shifted with the course of
World War I. Press reports from Petrograd, Berlin, and Stockholm
swiveled like weathervanes. So long as there was a chance Russia
would continue fighting Germany, the newspaper of record offered
readers a positive picture of the October Revolution. When it became
clear that the Bolsheviks would pull the new Soviet Union out of the
war, the "Red Peril" theme appeared in *The Times*'s foreign report, and
"organized propaganda for [U.S.] intervention penetrated the news."

"In the large, the news about Russia is a case of seeing not what
was, but what men wished to see," Lippmann and Merz concluded. A
little further on: "From the point of view of professional journalism
the reporting of the Russian Revolution is nothing short of a disas-
ter.... They were performing the supreme duty in a democracy of
supplying the information on which public opinion feeds, and they
were derelict in that duty." One could carry these judgments forward
to the post-Roosevelt half of the 1940s, and indeed to our age of raging
Russophobia, without altering a syllable.

Truman, easily influenced by the out-of-office Churchill and others closer to him, was waging the Cold War within weeks of assuming
the presidency, telling Vyacheslav Molotov, the Soviet foreign minister, he was ready to ignore Moscow's interests straight up to the
Soviets' borders as the U.S. began its quest for global preëminence.
In early 1947, Truman and Dean Acheson, his secretary of state, made
up their minds to support Greece's fascist monarchy, then facing a
popular front of multiple persuasions. This was Washington's first
postwar effort to intervene in the name of countering what it would
cavalierly call, over and over for the next four decades, Soviet aggression. George II and his successor, King Paul, were fighting a civil war,
but the democratic aspirations of Greeks counted not at all inside the
Truman administration.

The Truman Doctrine, by which the United States would award itself the right to undertake such interventions, was going to be a hard sell. There would be resistance on Capitol Hill to the four hundred million dollars (not quite five billion dollars today) the administration proposed to spend propping up a widely unpopular monarchy. Most Americans still aspired to F.D.R.'s plans for peaceable relations with the Soviets. Acheson, other State Department officials, and various congressional leaders labored long over the speech Truman was to give to a joint session of Congress on 12 March 1947. How should the Missouri haberdasher break the news that the dream of a peaceable world order was over? "It was still not possible," a State Department official named Louis Halle lamented at the time, "to tell the American people what the real issue was." The real issue, of course, was the limitless assertion of American power abroad and the kindling of another depleting era of hostility. Arthur Vandenberg, a Republican senator and a presence in the planning of America's postwar posture, offered advice that tumbles down to us, and for good reason: "Mr. President, the only way you are ever going to get this is to make a speech and scare hell out of the country."

Truman's speech had a shaky relationship with the truth, to put the point gently, but his scare-hell project proved a success. And it was at this point the American press made what was arguably among its most consequential decisions of the Cold War decades. There would have been no scaring hell out of anyone, Truman and Acheson might not have gotten their license to intervene, had it not been for the complicity of American newspapers and broadcasters. Coverage of the Greek crisis was supinely faithful to the Truman-Acheson whitewash—this to the point of covering up the assassination of one of American media's own, George Polk, a CBS News correspondent who was about to expose the Greek foreign minister for embezzling a considerable portion of that aid Truman advertised as crucial.

As Truman's speech reminds us, the Cold War's first front, where victory was essential to all other efforts, was at home—the battle for public opinion. Few Americans saw any chance of a third world war at the end of the second; neither did they want one. But by 1948, a Gallup poll indicated that three-quarters of the populace was braced for war in a necessary defense of "freedom." This was manufactured consent in unalloyed form. The Alsop brothers, Stewart and Joe, columnists and

Cold Warriors to the core, wrote in the *New York Herald Tribune* at the time, "The atmosphere in Washington today is no longer a post-war atmosphere. It is, to put it bluntly, a pre-war atmosphere." The task was simply to spread this atmosphere across the nation.

I must make special mention here of the role of television in conjuring this atmosphere: It was essential. Network television and Washington's first-generation Cold Warriors were co-dependents of a sort, having come into being more or less simultaneously. The new networks—CBS, NBC, ABC, and DuMont—were paupers next to what the big three have become. They had little experience in news-gathering and next to none on the foreign side. Nervous advertisers, reticent to sponsor programs that might be even marginally controversial, had considerable power over what was broadcast. Credibility was also in short supply: Among much of the public, and certainly among journalists, television news was taken as an adjunct of entertainment.

Collaborating with government agencies offered a way past these handicaps. They produced and supplied programming, enabling news departments to broadcast "news" on the cheap. Officially sanctioned material eased anxieties among advertisers and sponsors and made news divisions look sound and serious. For the government agencies, notably public affairs offices in the State and Defense departments, this was the best thing to come along since TV dinners (which first graced suburban dining tables in 1948). If it was early days for television, the new medium would soon be powerful, as wiser heads at the networks and in government were early to understand. It would have exceptional reach into Americans' living rooms—and so into their minds, given it made widely available those most insidious and manipulable of propaganda devices, images.

From 1948 to 1954, as Nancy Bernhard tells us in *U.S. Television News and Cold War Propaganda*, this partnership amounted to "a joint, public-private propaganda operation." I see no other way to characterize this arrangement. Among its first products was *The Armed Forces Hour*, broadcast weekly from 1949 to 1951, first by NBC and subsequently by DuMont. Numerous other programs of this kind followed—*America at Mid-Century* (NBC), *The Marshall Plan in Action* (ABC, renamed *Strength for a Free World*), *World Briefing* (CBS, later called *Diplomatic Pouch*), and so on. Government agencies produced or coproduced these programs and handed them over for broadcast. By the mid-fifties, news divisions having found their feet, the government role shifted from producer to close collaborator, still with considerable control over programming. The networks' task was to make these productions appear independent, probing, scrupulously objective. With the Cold War the nation's new reality, propaganda was widely accepted in these circles as essential to the conduct of foreign policy. Even those most stubbornly dedicated to a free press came to believe in the necessity of official control of information.

This marked a decisive turn in American thinking. America possessed the truth, and the truth was all it needed, for the truth was ever invincible: This was fundamental to the nation's self-image. Now this belief gave way to a new conviction that the truth was not enough in the face of "the Communist menace." Soviet propaganda had to be countered with superior propaganda. In a 1950 speech to American newspaper editors, Truman called this dimension of the Cold War "the Campaign of Truth." It was an early but still exceptional example of the language Orwell called Newspeak in his celebrated *1984*, published but one year earlier. Gaining public support for American policy, Acheson later wrote in *Present at the Creation*, required the government to make its case "clearer than the truth."

There was a subliminal power to television, an acculturating power, we must also note. The appearance of news broadcasts in a thoroughly commercialized society embedded them in the postwar culture of material plentitude and voracious consumption. Airing opposite *I Love Lucy* and the *Milton Berle Show* further identified televised news with what Bernhard calls "a consumer's Cold War." The finesse with which news divisions obscured their ties to government propaganda operations, as the government's public affairs officials insisted they do, greatly enhanced the effort. Americans needed the illusion of free, independent networks and averted their eyes to preserve it, while television sold policy the way Bucky Beaver sold Ipana toothpaste. The pose of objectivity was essential. Theatrical simulations of detached professionalism naturalized—Bernhard's term—Cold War ideology and what we now call Russsophobia as objective realities, part of the American experience just as much as the *Colgate Comedy Hour* and Rice Krispies' Snap, Crackle, and Pop.

If the press was subtler than the broadcasters in its relations to the national security state, it was equally faithful to the new cause, its exuberant anti-Communism tipping not infrequently into the extremes those who lived through the Cold War commonly recall. From a generous inventory of such material, I select a takeout *Look* published on 3 August 1948 under the headline, "Could the Reds Seize Detroit?" This piece is exemplary of its time. "Detroit is the industrial heart of America," the writer begins. "Today, a sickle is being sharpened to plunge into that heart.... The Reds are going boldly about their business." Before he finishes, James Metcalfe—let this byline be recorded—has Motor City besieged in "an all-out initial blow in the best blitzkrieg fashion." The presentation featured masked Communists murdering police officers and telephone operators, seizing airports, blowing up bridges, power grids, rail lines, and highways. "Caught in the madness of the moment, emboldened by the darkness, intoxicated by an unbridled license to kill and loot, mobs would swarm the streets." Communist mobs, naturally.

While the more august dailies eschewed this sort of material, the difference was in large measure a matter of style. Major and minor newspapers, the wire services, the broadcasters—all assumed masks of authoritative objectivity to elevate fear among Americans to a condition of normalized frenzy. The press devastated Joe McCarthy as his bubble of paranoia was bursting, but—let this be very clear—there would have been no moment in the sun for the Wisconsin senator had the media not fed his campaign against "Reds" everywhere.

Innocents are hard to find in accounts of this period. Purges of fellow travelers and others suspected of harboring Communist sympathies—and suspicion, rumor, or innuendo would often do—were common in the mainstream press. In 1947 three former FBI agents founded American Business Consultants, an operation fronting for vigorously anti-Communist corporate executives and former federal bureaucrats. Three years later they published the infamous *Red Channels*, a newsletter that blacklisted one hundred fifty-one broadcast journalists and entertainers, including William Shirer and Howard K. Smith, leaving many lives and careers in ruins. It was scoundrel time, as Lillian Hellman later put it in her memoir of this name. By the mid-fifties, all major news organizations were serving as the information appendages of the government. The networks were the extreme case, but the fateful bond forged during these years between media and the emergent national security state extended across the board.

The harm American media did themselves as they chose this direction is hard to overstate. Their independence from power had rarely been what it ought to have been, but even this collapsed during the Cold War crusade. Apart from all the corrupted copy and television news clips, journalists became hopelessly confused in matters of patriotism. The assumption creeping in along with the Cold War atmosphere was that journalists were Americans, too, and should serve the national cause as would any other citizen. I still cannot fathom this reasoning. It seems never to have occurred to most reporters and editors that to be a good American one needed only to be a good reporter or editor.

Kennedy gave this error a sharp edge shortly after the Bay of Pigs fiasco in April 1961. Tad Szulc, a seasoned *Times* correspondent, had uncovered the CIA's covert training work among Cuban exiles while on a visit to Miami. His piece ran on 7 April 1961, ten days before the invasion, but not before Turner Catledge, the managing editor at the time, gutted Szulc's detailed reporting and all mention of the CIA, leaving the impression that Washington's hands were clean. Addressing a group of editors gathered at the White House, Kennedy turned to Catledge. "Maybe if you had printed more about the operation," he admonished the courtly Southerner, "you would have saved us from a colossal mistake."

The moment merits consideration. Kennedy was famously at odds with Allen Dulles, the CIA's director, and considered his attempted invasion of Cuba recklessly bold. In confronting Catledge, Kennedy was clearly intent on castigating what was then the newspaper of record for neglecting its duty to report on institutions of power while standing independently of them. But Kennedy wanted it more ways than one. When he finished chiding Catledge and addressed the gathering, he proposed an editorial standard any serious journalist would have to count corrupt. Before going to press with a story, he told the assembled, *Is it news?* is not the only question to be asked. *Is it in the interest of national security?* must also be considered. This was an invitation to the American press, embarrassingly forthright, to confirm its loyalty to the Cold War cause. Keep the faith despite the mess we just made: This was Kennedy's point. Not until September 2001 was there a more explicit request for the media to breach one of its fundamental principles. On both occasions—the second to be considered in pages to come—the decision to cooperate was unanimous.

The unspoken question that day concerned self-censorship. The American press was well-versed in this regrettable skill before Truman and the media sold the Cold War to the American populace. Journalists had long earlier learned to hide their shadows and hide from them, to put this point another way. But the censors in reporters' and editors' heads consolidated their power in the early postwar years. It was commonly asserted, then as now, that private ownership protected the press and broadcasters from the state controls found in the Soviet Union, China, and the East bloc nations. This was and remains true only in the very narrowest sense. Intimate relationships such as those I have here described blurred the lines between media and the national security state. There was indeed no overt censorship in America, but there was no need of any. Everyone in the profession understood where the fence posts were, as do all journalists now.

In fairness to our newspapers and broadcasters, I have often wondered whether Americans are singularly given to an excessive regard for orthodoxies and if our media serve merely as a mirror. "In America the majority raises formidable barriers around freedom of opinion," de Tocqueville wrote in volume one of *Democracy in America*. "Within these barriers an author may write what he pleases, but woe to him if he goes beyond them." The thought is nearly two hundred years old. We are left to ask if the press's Cold War performance could have been any different—or if it simply reflected back on Americans what they have been from the beginning. The lead weight of conformity: Few of us have ever seemed able or even inclined to lift it.

O N 9 JANUARY 1953, *The Washington Post* published an editorial we can read all these years later as a murmur amid silence. "Choice or Chance" was a blunt worry about what the CIA, five years old at this time, was getting up to. Was the agency to analyze information it gathered or that had come to it—a matter of chance—or was it actively and covertly to execute interventions of its own choosing? The agency hardly invented clandestine operations, coups, assassinations, disinformation campaigns, election fixing, bribery in high places, false flags, and the like. But it was elaborating and institutionalizing such intrigues, and they were coming to define America's Cold War conduct. *The Post* stood with the objectors—at least it did on page twenty of that winter Friday's editions. The agency's activities were "incompatible with a democracy," Washington's local paper protested. They risked an unwanted war. Reform was in order. Once again to be noted: The conflict *The Post* aired concerned method. The Cold War's taxonomy and Washington's division of the world into adversarial blocs lay beyond question.

As interesting as *The Post*'s editorial was the dead quiet that followed. Nothing more was published on the topic. Eight months later, *The Post* obfuscated the CIA's role in the coup that toppled the Mossadegh government in Iran; a year after that came the coup that brought down the democratically elected government of Jacobo Árbenz in Guatemala, and the CIA's role in it was once again illegible. Operating with little inhibition, the agency would later plot to plant an exploding cigar in Castro's humidor and make a pornographic film with a look-alike actor impersonating Sukarno, Indonesia's too-independent president (later deposed in a CIA-cultivated coup). American readers and viewers knew next to nothing of all such operations, as intended. Nor did they seem to want to. Citizens were willingly transformed into consumers. A national somnambulance had set in.

Nineteen fifty-three was a peculiar year for *The Post* to question the CIA's drift into activist intrigues. Allen Dulles took over as the agency's director less than a month after *The Post* editorial appeared. Dulles put Frank Wisner, a former OSS man, in charge of the agency's "black operations." This included making maximum use of the press by compromising its ranks—not least its high command. Journalists were recruited to serve as agents, agents were trained sufficiently to pose as journalists, not infrequently with the blessings of publishers and network presidents. Wisner called his operation "my mighty Wurlitzer" after those turn-of-the-century contraptions that performed musical magic at the strike of a key.

The more alert reporters, correspondents, and editors had long suspected there were CIA operatives in their midst. There was no evidence of this, and, then as now, one did not name a name without any. A silence worthy of a Catholic chapel prevailed for two decades after Wisner set his machine in motion. When this was finally broken, it was as a pebble tossed into a pond produces ever-larger ripples.

Jack Anderson, the iconoclastic columnist, revealed in the autumn of 1973, just as I was crossing the marble floor at *The News*, that a Hearst Newspapers reporter had spied on Democratic presidential candidates in the service of the Nixon campaign. At the time Anderson published, Seymour Frieden was a Hearst correspondent in London. Not quite in passing but nearly, Anderson also reported that Frieden tacitly acknowledged working for the CIA.

The pebble was tossed. The ripples grew slowly at first.

William Colby, the recently named director of the CIA, responded with a standard agency maneuver: When news is going to break against you, disclose the minimum, bury the rest, and maintain control of what we now call "the narrative." Among the spooks this was and remains known as a "limited hangout." Colby "leaked" to a *Washington Star-News* reporter named Oswald Johnston. Johnston's piece was fronted on 30 November 1973. "The Central Intelligence Agency," it began, "has some three dozen American journalists working abroad on its payroll as undercover informants, some of them full-time agents, the *Star-News* has learned." Johnston followed this four-square lead just as Colby had wished. "Colby is understood to have ordered the termination of this handful of journalist-agents," he wrote further down in his report, adding—and this is the truly delightful part—"on the full realization that CIA employment of reporters in a nation which prides itself on an independent press is a subject fraught with controversy." Johnston broke a big story, Johnston was a patsy. This was the agency's "tradecraft" in action.

Once again, the rest of the press let Johnston's revelations sink without further investigation. But Colby's gambit was on the way to failing, as was the press's see-no-evil pose. A year after the Johnston piece appeared, Stuart Loory, a former *Los Angeles Times* correspondent and then a journalism professor at The Ohio State University, published a piece in the *Columbia Journalism Review* that stands as the first extensive exploration of relations between the CIA and the press. Another year later, the CIA found itself where it never wanted to be: in the public eye, visible.

Even before it was over, 1975 was known as "the Year of Intelligence." In January, President Ford commissioned a committee to investigate the CIA's illegal breaches. Soon after Ford named his experts, among them none other than Ronald Reagan, the Senate and

House convened their own committees to look into the CIA's doings abroad and at home. The Church Committee, so named for Frank Church, an Idaho Democrat who headed the Senate inquiry, was the committee that mattered. Its final report arrived in six volumes in April 1976, the Year of Intelligence proving a long one.

This was a critical moment for America's Cold War edifice—or it could have been, I had better put it. The Church Committee was to be the first concerted attempt to exert political control over an agency that had long since, as we say now, "gone rogue." In this, Church and his investigative staff held the making of history in their hands. They could have deprived those asserting America's global hegemony one of their most essential institutions, and they would have decisively cut media's ties with it. As things turned out, the Church Committee's failure is wherein the history resides. In the breach, those directing the undertaking elected to obfuscate the obfuscators.

Ties of all sorts to journalists of all sorts were among the programs the CIA was most vigorously determined to keep in the shadows. The agency's elisions, untruths, and arms-folded refusals to cooperate with Senate investigators must count as a model for all aspiring stonewallers. In due course, the Church Committee found itself drawn into prolonged negotiations with Colby and other senior CIA officials it never should have entered upon. There were other indicators that failure was on the way. The committee had spent too much time on assassination plots and agency exotica to give the question of press complicity the attention it warranted. Church, who for a time nursed dreams of a run for the presidency, did not want his name on an investigation that would make a faux-patriotic agency protecting national security look as objectionable as it was.

The final "findings" found little to find. No one from the press was called to testify—no correspondents, no editors, none of those at the top of the major dailies or the broadcasters. A year after the committee released its six volumes, Carl Bernstein of Watergate fame elicited in eight words all that needed saying about the sixteen months of Capitol Hill drama. Faced with the prospect of forcing the CIA to sever all covert ties with the press, a senator Bernstein did not name remarked, "We just weren't ready to take that step."

It was Bernstein who unwrapped the story. In a twenty-five thousand word piece published in *Rolling Stone* on 20 October 1977, the ex–*Post* reporter led readers into a vast universe of connections, co-optation, and collusion. It wasn't "some three dozen journalists operating as agents." It was more than four hundred. All the names were there: *The Times*, *The Post*, CBS, ABC, NBC, *Newsweek*, *TIME*, the wires. Those cooperating ran to the top: William Paley (CBS), Arthur Hays and C. L. Sulzberger (*The Times*), the Alsop brothers (the *New York Herald Tribune*, later *The Washington Post*). Arthur Hays Sulzberger, *The Times*'s publisher, had a signed a secrecy agreement with the CIA and gave his tacit approval to correspondents who wanted to work for the agency. Seymour Hersh and I. F. Stone, two exemplary independent journalists at this time, had also reported on the CIA's numerous illegal programs, known in-house as "the family jewels." It was Hersh who, in December 1974, broke the story of the agency's extravagant spying operations focused on antiwar activists and other dissidents—a seven-thousand-word piece that prefigured the Church Committee by a month and five days, But Bernstein's mastery of detail on the agency's penetration of the press—too profuse to recount but briefly—remains nonpareil. Most of it derived from CIA files and interviews with agency officials and the journalists the Church Committee never asked to testify.

In what coverage there was of the decades of deceit, the press did its best to convey the impression it was the unscrupulously sullied innocent. Most of those involved professed to know nothing about all the consensual compromises. Some were proudly patriotic. "I've done things for them when I thought they were the right thing to do," Joe Alsop told Bernstein. "I call it doing my duty as a citizen." But lapsed memories, lies, and blurred lines were the prevalent responses. While a CIA officer described C. L. Sulzberger as "very eager" to cooperate with the agency, Cy told Bernstein he "would never get caught near the spook business." Working for the agency and never getting caught working for it seem to have been two different things in Cy's mind.

The Church Committee left various marks on the record. Some relationships between Langley and the media were broken off as the committee shut up shop. Things were not so openly and incautiously corrupt as they had been pre-Church. This was also the beginning of a long decline in mainstream media's credibility, which, to be honest, I consider a healthy thing. But the Senate investigation stands in hindsight as an early example of that political event we now know too well: It was spectacle. This was how all sides wished it to be. The Wurlitzer's volume was turned down. But as that anonymous senator said so simply, nobody ever intended to unplug it.

It would be supremely naïve to assume the Wurlitzer does not play in our time, leaving us to live with the Church Committee's purposeful failing, as we must count it. The agency's immunity from all oversight is now inviolable. What Capitol Hill committee now would dare to hold hearings such as those that gave the Year of Intelligence its name? Langley's ties to the press are a closed book. *Wikipedia*, the alternative encyclopedia with its own objectionable relations with intelligence, as we speak carries this sentence in its entry on the Cold War programs: "By the time the Church Committee Report was completed, all CIA contacts with accredited journalists had been dropped." This is patently, demonstrably false.

I recount very briefly the evil that supposedly passed. This is the foundation on which many American myths rest. The press and broadcasters still crouch behind this one.

INDIA'S "FREEDOM AT MIDNIGHT" in 1947 began "the independence era," when scores of new nations broke the colonial bond. This swift turn of history's wheel was of great consequence for America as it rose to postwar preëminence. Its inheritance was not what the policy cliques in Washington had anticipated after the 1945 victories: The presumption of Western superiority, half a millennium old, was beginning to end. The elites shaping and running policy in Washington began to see what they wanted to see, as Lippmann and Merz had found decades earlier. This is why so many of the CIA's covert operations during this time were aimed at third world liberation movements and the legitimately elected governments of very young nations.

So it was that Washington set out to shape reality to its wishes. The Dulles brothers—Allen as CIA director, John Foster as secretary of state—are commonly assigned responsibility for this turn against the world as it was becoming. Both entertained remarkable delusions about the nation's power, place, and prerogative. But they were hardly alone. They expressed a confident and profoundly anxious nation all at once. If we assign to them a certain kind of psychosis, the policy cliques drifted into this condition along with them early in the postwar years. The American media's cooperation in this project marked a turn that cannot be overstated for its consequences. If we define psychosis as a defective relationship with external reality, the press's assigned task was to make sure Americans suffered from it.

Edward R. Murrow addressed this question in a speech to television news directors in the autumn of 1958. "If there are any historians about fifty or a hundred years from now and there should be preserved the Kinescopes for one week of all three networks," he remarked, "they will there find recorded in black and white or color evidence of decadence, escapism, and insulation from the realities of the world in which we live." Murrow, a scarred veteran of television's ethical blur by this time, was already falling from favor among colleagues, and his speech further alienated him: It was too pithily to the point. To insulate Americans from reality became the work of media altogether during the Cold War decades.

In "Lying in Politics: Reflections on the Pentagon Papers," published in *The New York Review of Books* in 1971, Hannah Arendt termed this slide into collective psychosis, which is a term I think it fair to use, "defactualization." Facts are fragile, Arendt wrote, in that they tell no story in themselves, a little in the way a stone in the road has no story to tell. This leaves them vulnerable to the manipulations of storytellers. "The deliberate falsehood deals with *contingent* facts," Arendt explained in this remarkable piece of work, "that is, with matters which carry no inherent truth within themselves, no necessity to be as they are; factual truths are never compellingly true." The facts don't speak for themselves, the folk wisdom notwithstanding.

It is a subtle but essential thought. A departure from reason, from factual assessment, was long evident by the time Arendt wrote. A few years after "Lying in Politics" appeared, Arthur Miller published the searching reminiscence from which I quoted earlier. He called it "The Year It Came Apart." The playwright's reference was to 1949, though his intent was to explain the American condition in the mid-nineteen seventies. "A sort of political surrealism came dancing through the ruins of what had nearly been a beautifully moral and rational world," Miller wrote plaintively. "Nothing could any longer be what it seemed." This was precisely the point as a culture of concealment and deception spread through all ranks of government. Creating and preserving a winning image of America had become the primary pursuit. With the Vietnam War going badly, selling imagery was key to the prosecution of foreign policy by this time. Those reading newspapers or watching television news were "audience," as Arendt had observed. "Scenarios" that preserved the appearance of American innocence and honor were all. "Perception management," as we put it now, was elevated to a status near to a *scienza nuova.*

Americans had been ushered into a state of ignorance—I do not have another word for it—since the national security state took shape in the early Cold War years. In time they began to lose all ability to see or think clearly about the world around them. So did the press come to tip its very purpose upside down. It is mistake enough to surrender independence, drastically narrowing the difference between the major American dailies and *Pravda.* It is altogether another to cooperate with a government as it shrouds itself in "an Alice-in-Wonderland atmosphere"—a phrase from Arendt's essay. This landed the press in the alternative-reality business. Informing opinion became manipulating opinion. To abandon reality: It is difficult to imagine a more fundamental betrayal of what newspapers and broadcasters owe their public.

Certain malign practices any honest journalist will acknowledge were common features of the Cold War compromises I outline. High among them is what is called "the access game," which is played with singular vigor in Washington. There is one rule: Write to reflect well upon your sources if you want to keep those sources—even if they are in "defactualization" mode. Tom Wicker, who had a long and principled career at *The New York Times*, was an outspoken critic of the practice by the early nineteen sixties, arguing that good journalism required reporters to accept the risk of falling out of favor among their sources. Implicit in this are assumptions of equity and a proper distance between reporter and reported upon. But Wicker's was a voice in the wilderness. From his day to ours, and with admirable but few exceptions, preserving access has taken priority over what a reporter might know full well should be written.

The preoccupation with access produced another game I took many years ago to calling POLO, the power of leaving out. One could find lies in the major dailies during the Cold War—as one can now, indeed. But published untruths and distortions risk revelation. Lies of omission—trafficking in selective facts while leaving unmentioned those that would make a given story genuinely accurate—leave nothing on paper and can be just as effective when the intent is to mislead. So has POLO taken its place alongside the access game as common practice in American journalism since the Cold War decades.

The Cold War required a language of its own. Just as Louis Halle observed as the Truman Doctrine took shape, it was simply not possible to tell Americans the truth of America's new enterprise. The result, in government and in the press, was the cotton-wool language of obfuscation, as I call it. During my *Daily News* years, I learned the value of clarity as if it were the fourth theological virtue. I soon recognized the corresponding effect of language when put to insidious purpose. "The greatest enemy of clear language is insincerity," Orwell wrote in "Politics and the English Language"—an essay that, appearing in 1946, could not have better suited the time. "When there is a gap between one's real and declared aims, one turns as it were to long words and exhausted idioms." Corrupt thought corrupts language and corrupt language thought—this was roughly Orwell's argument, and it is precisely mine. Events turn into abstractions as they are conveyed to readers. Reality is rendered indistinct. The drift away from clear language, beginning in Washington's corridors and emanating into newsrooms, was key to making America's Cold War conduct acceptable to the public. Our major dailies are still written in cotton-wool language, *The New York Times* the long-established master of the practice.

Easy it is to deplore the Cold War's extremes—the *Look* and *LIFE* takeouts, the delusions of Cold War columnists, the adulterous relations with the CIA, the routine corruptions I have just noted. We must take care not to deceive ourselves. What we now recognize as a kind of madness did not seem so at the time. Turning this thought over, few recognize the madness of our time as such. Much that afflicts American media now arose from the delusions and illusions of the past. They have never broken out of the self-neutering proximity to power they eagerly sought during the Cold War: This is documented history, but it is also our present circumstance.

It was evident by the time I found my way into the craft that the press was having a bad Cold War. And I saw little prospect of recovery, even then, without some major impetus to break with the past. Like the Washington policy elites the major dailies and network covered, they could not learn from their mistakes, those greatest of teachers, because they could not bear to face them. With this refusal, American newspapers and broadcasters abdicated any prospect of achieving a transcendent grasp of their time and the structures of power within which they had come to serve. They were unable to see over the walls they had helped construct.

I wasn't interested in walls but for the thought of breaking them down when occasions arose, or climbing over them.

DURING MY YEARS at *The News,* I got to know a copy editor named Bill Dunlap. Full-bearded, long-haired, and with an easy, beaming smile, Bill had a touch of the disaffected about him in the mode of the time. He was an excellent line editor, but Bill was as alienated at *The News* as I was. He eventually left the paper to study law. At writing he still professes at a university in southern Connecticut.

We used to lunch at a *prix fixe* place in the East Thirties called Bienvenue. Over one of these, in the Indian summer of 1974, he told me he spent a couple of mornings a week proofreading pages at the *Guardian,* a weekly long known for its left-handed politics. The paper was a mainstay of the antiwar movement, and proofing its pages was Bill's contribution to the effort. I sat up and listened. It seemed to me there might be something there for my wandering spirit. In time Bill introduced me, and I, too, began correcting proofs on the hectic days before the paper went out to the printer.

A door had opened. It led into the independent press as it was then.

I still recall arriving that first day at the *Guardian*'s offices off Union Square. The building was one of those sooted edifices erected to accommodate blouse factories, assemblers of plastic toys, and who knew how many other small-time manufacturers. No brass-bound world map in a marble floor this time. A rattling freight elevator lined with quilted blankets carried me to the paper's ninth-floor loft. I stepped off into a warren of cramped rooms—circulation here, typesetting there, the mailroom somewhere behind both. The newsroom was a disheveled space at the rear brightened by immense north- and east-facing windows. It was lined with books and files that had the look of an archive in need of an archivist. The floor creaked pleasantly, as they do in those old buildings. The desks, apart from plywood-and-filing-cabinet improvisations, were of scarred wood and dated, surely, to the late forties, when the paper first appeared as the *National Guardian.* I must have derived some subliminal meaning from the trappings and the dust and cigarette smoke that lingered in the morning sunlight, it occurs to me now. They suggested a tradition worth honoring, allowing the thought that I might add to it in the way Gropius had written of the architecture at Harvard.

To know the *Guardian*'s history was to recognize it among the remarkable endeavors of twentieth-century journalism. Cedric Belfrage and James Aronson, an expatriate Englishman and an American, conceived of an independent newspaper, immune from the corruptions they knew well, while serving in occupied Germany. The two were assigned to de-Nazify the press and rebuild a news-paper culture suited to a newly democratic nation—"journalism run by journalists," as Aronson put it. The paper Belfrage and Aronson eventually published back in America came out in support of the pres-idential campaign of Henry Wallace, who ran against Truman in 1948 on a Progressive Party ticket. But party affiliation was pointedly not the point. Sound journalism was the point. Here are extracts from a statement of intent that ran in the 18 October 1948 edition, the paper's premiere. Belfrage, Aronson, and Jack McManus, recruited to run the business side, signed it:

> We present our publication humbly, in the conviction that the times call for a voice in our nation which without fear or reservation will bespeak the cause of peace, freedom, and abundance…. The need for continuing, progressive publication devoted to these ideals becomes one of the most pressing needs of our time.

These lines were published just as America was about to tip into Arthur's Miller's "year it came apart." By 1948, the anti-Communist *folie Américaine* was spreading like kudzu across the landscape. But as Miller mourned the fading hopes of a different time, the *National Guardian* held resolutely to them. Of official harassment there would be plenty in the years to come. But nobody seems to have flinched in the borrowed offices near City Hall where the paper first bivouacked.

Money was to be tight the whole of the paper's life. But Belfrage and Aronson had struck a vein. In a way good historians would be first to understand, they had brought to the surface a counter-tradition in journalism that was as old and as American as the republic. Subscriptions poured in, as did job applications and stories from hundreds of reporters. In time, the *National Guardian*'s contributors included an extraordinary gathering of political, cultural, and literary figures, among them Miller, Norman Mailer, W. E. B. Du Bois, Sean O'Casey, William Appleman Williams, Eugene Genovese, Staughton Lynd, Maxwell Geismar, Tom Hayden, and Wilfred Burchett, a well-traveled correspondent who was to cover the world's biggest stories for the next three and some decades.

What green aspirant wouldn't want to add his byline to such an assembly—literate, politically engaged, above all dedicated to a journalism of integrity? The appeal moved fewer as the years went on, in truth. *National Guardian* pay was lean and the life precarious. By the 1950s most journalists were professionalized in the way I have previously used this term. Dreams of status at the elite end of the middle class and a life inside the tent rather than beyond it nearly always extinguished the flame burning within many newcomers to the craft. I still find it remarkable—and difficult to explain to those not in newspapers—how second-home mortgages, school bills, BMWs, and European holidays can determine the way the most momentous world events are reported.

I resisted when my time came. As I stepped off the elevator at 33 West Seventeenth Street, I stepped into something of a floating world, as the Japanese would call it. Independent media then were in the way of transient, uncertain, struggling for stability, the best of them nonetheless thoughtful and fully alive to the world in which we lived. I followed my feet when I took the subway south from Forty-Second Street to Union Square. In one of its dimensions this book is the story of where they have led me.

T HE *NATIONAL GUARDIAN'S* circulation reached seventy-six thousand by the end of its second year, a measure of the peaceable postwar mood. Then the Cold War inquisition began to exact its toll and the strong momentum was interrupted. Cedric Belfrage, not yet naturalized, was deported in 1955, having testified uncooperatively before McCarthy's Senate subcommittee two years earlier. This left Jim Aronson to run the newsroom. He did so for twelve more years. At that point it wasn't Cold Warriors or FBI informants (of which more than a few) who dealt the paper a critical blow. The New Left was by then dividing itself into "fissions without end," as Belfrage put it later. The *National Guardian* soon had a case of this wasteful madness.

The transformation of some of the *National Guardian*'s staff into sophomoric dreamers with just enough history in their heads to miss its meaning entirely was evident by the mid-sixties. They made the not-uncommon mistake of confusing journalism and activism. Aronson and Belfrage, "editor-in-exile" since he settled in Mexico, were effectively ousted. They submitted their resignations on the same day in April 1967. The *National Guardian*, "the progressive news-weekly," became the *Guardian*, "independent radical newsweekly." In the years that followed, the lapse of the left into a Surreal sectarianism grew ever further from reality. To anyone gazing into those large loft windows the newsroom would have seemed like some sort of snow globe scene—silent, hermetic, distant, wholly other.

The legacy Belfrage and Aronson left behind still lingered in the air with all the dust as I marked my proofs. I shared with a number of others a professional regard for what an independent press could accomplish in the name of the paper's ideals, although we understood that Belfrage and Aronson's New Deal-ish sensibilities no longer suited our time. In the course of things Cedric and I became friends by mail, he still resident in Cuernavaca. I sent him a copy of *The American Inquisition*, his just-published book on the McCarthy period, and he returned it signed with a note. "Yes, I still get the *Guardian*," it reads, "but I see no future for ideological virgins, and am bored by the struggle among Marxist-Leninist sects while Rome burns around us." I drew comfort from this distant friend and his "fraternal *abrazo*."

The weekly foreign report had always been among the paper's strong suits and was relatively untouched by the cardboard ideological allegiances. This mattered to me, for my interest had already turned to international affairs. Jack Smith, the paper's editor, was a curious figure—a resolute ideologue with a delightful sense of humor. He shared my interest in foreign news. He was very taken with the Chinese Revolution—too given to the romance of it to see it in full—but he had been a hardheaded deskman and a reporter at United Press International in a previous lifetime. Jack understood I was there for the journalism, not the activism. He also valued the standards I brought downtown from the *Daily News*.

One day as I sat at the proofing desk, Jack asked me to pick up my extension and take dictation. It was a bright spring morning, and the sun streamed onto my pages through one of the east-facing windows. The call was from Wilfred Burchett, who I knew only by name and reputation. He had distinguished himself many times over since covering World War II, most recently as the only Western correspondent to report the Vietnam War from the North. He did so on a bicycle in áo *bà ba*, what we insist on calling "black pajamas." Wilfred was calling from Lisbon this time. Portugal had had its Revolution of Carnations in April 1974, when army officers serving in the failing African colonies returned to topple Marcelo Caetano's dilapidated dictatorship, then a half-century old. A year later Wilfred was covering the pitched political battles that would set the nation's new course. There was talk—wildly overblown per Cold War custom—of a Soviet foothold in southern Europe. This was Wilfred, there at whatever "there" was running on page one.

He was a genial, earthy Australian, cultured but with no shred of pretense about him. I still recall that first collaboration by telephone. I knew instantly there was a professional, in the better meaning of the term, at the other end of the line. Wilfred read in his worn-smooth accent, slowly enough for me to keep pace at the typewriter. He had a singular way with proper names. Melo Antunes (theoretician of the Captains' Coup, as the military overthrow was also called) came out "Meeehlllloooh Aaanntuuunneeehjjj" in lilting cadences. Vasco Gonçalves (another officer and premier in the first provisional government) arrived in my headphones as "Vaaahssscoooh Gonnsaaahlllveeehjjj." Wilfred must have acquired this considerate habit over the course of a thousand telephone dictations.

I didn't edit Wilfred's Lisbon file. I neatened up my typed pages, walked them over to Jack, and returned to my proofing. There are rare occasions in fortunately lived young lives when one is visited by a premonition of things to come, the path out front illuminated. So it seems to have been that morning. I knew then I was to live my life, or a good part of it, as a correspondent abroad. Wilfred was shortly to leave Lisbon. My quiet epiphany: I don't know how else to explain the determination, unmarked by doubt, that drove me from that day forward to follow the route he had opened to me—in the first instance literally.

Everything now turned to my new plan. At *The News*, I spent long hours in the morgue photocopying years of Portugal coverage in all the major dailies. I sold all I owned of any worth, cameras and darkroom gear mostly, for I had been taking photographs for several years. I had my Royal Speed King, a hand-me-down from my father, cleaned and re-ribboned. Jack agreed to write letters of accreditation, essential equipment for any arriving correspondent. In the late spring of 1975, I resigned from *The News*, stuffed a suitcase with clothes and clippings, said goodbye to my beloved, and flew to Paris. Life took on the look of those bright, beckoning flowerbeds in the Jardin des Tuileries.

It never takes much to get me to pass through Paris, but there was purpose in my stop this time. Wilfred lived with his wife, Vessa, and their children in Meudon, a western suburb halfway between Paris and Versailles. I knew he wouldn't be there: Jack had told me he was on his way to cover the post-independence conflict in Angola, where another Cold War confrontation had ignited. But Wilfred had written the first of what turned out to be two Portugal books in no time, as was his gift. *The Captains' Coup* hadn't yet been published, but the typescript was in Meudon: Could I ask for a better primer explaining the stormy political sea I was about to plunge into?

I checked into l'Hôtel de l'Université, my Latin Quarter standby, and telephoned Mme. Burchett to see about the book. She greeted me with the wary frost I had fully anticipated. It is the only copy, she replied when I proposed spending a few days making notes on Wilfred's text. She wasn't sure Wilfred would approve. It was unwise, she pondered, to let the typescript out of the house. Finally: Could I telephone again tomorrow? I was sure she would call New York to see about this out-of-nowhere fellow and his importunate request.

Jack must've done the necessary. I took the train from the Gare Montparnasse the next morning, and on my arrival Vessa greeted me in the front garden with the typescript. I returned to Paris and spent the next few days at café tables filling several schoolboy's *cahiers* with what, when done, was a fulsome summary of Wilfred's book. When

I brought it back, Vessa offered a sparing smile. On the return train to Paris, I reflected that it was large and decent of Wilfred's wife, with an eyebrow rightfully arched, to trust me as she had. This was another of the Cold War's small corners: It draped blankets of doubt over otherwise ordinary encounters. Nothing, as Arthur Miller had foretold, was necessarily as it seemed.

*The Captains' Coup* was published in Lisbon later that year as *Portugal depois da Revolução dos Capitães* (Portugal since the Captains' Revolution). But it has never appeared in English. My *cahiers* are long lost and so, it seems, is the typescript. A professor in Boston, still trying to locate a copy of Wilfred's pages to bring out the book in its original, tells me I am very likely the only one to have read *The Captains' Coup* as Wilfred wrote it. This is unfortunate. It was a good account of unfolding events and their context.

I crossed Spain during what turned out to be the Franco regime's final months. A more downcast people I had never seen as my train, a cheap local, stopped in more stations than I could count. At each, Guardias Civiles with machine guns boarded briefly to walk the aisles, heads swiveling from side to side. Another bitter taste of the Cold War: This was my first glimpse of a dictatorship Washington counted an ally, the Falangist Franco having won its approval when, decades earlier, he took down the Spanish Republic. I learned quickly from the other passengers to keep my gaze averted and peel my oranges in silence.

Crossing into Portugal at Vilar Formoso and training through Coimbra, the celebrated university town, I was a stranger arriving at a boisterous party. The decades under António Salazar and then Caetano had left Lisbon looking like something out of a García Márquez novel—a *fin de siècle* backwater smothered in *saudade* and Iberian Catholicism. But dozens of political parties and *movimentos* had sprouted like spring flowers in the year since the revolution—so many I kept a list with notes as to the persuasions of each. A collective embrace of unfamiliar freedoms gave the effect of Jack springing out of his box. The Rossio, beating heart of the capital, was crowded with stalls offering everything from pornography to party banners on sticks to a vast variety of well- and badly done newspapers fighting their political corners on each *página um*. The political chatter began at sunrise and went on well into the evening.

Lisbon was my classroom. Most mornings I descended on the funicular from my *pensão* on rua Dom Pedro V, took espresso just off the Rossio, and planned the day: What press conferences, what rallies or demonstrations, what briefings, what interviews, what speeches? All was improvisation, nothing of the nation's future decided. As I made my way around the country, the state of near-total uncertainty I found seemed to me a rare and salutary interim. So fundamental a condition rendered people acutely alive. A kind of power falls to those courageous enough to accept that their future remains to be determined and lies in their hands. I, too, found a vitality in the life around me I have seldom known since.

But what the Portuguese called the *verão quente*, the hot summer, was soon upon us. There was a rightist coup attempt against the Gonçalves government in the spring. When it failed the Socialists started a destabilizing campaign of demonstrations against *"Vasco, Vasco, companheiro,"* as the prime minister's loyal supporters shouted at their gatherings. Another coup attempt, known as *25 de Novembro* for its date, would make the point plain: Portugal had scores of political formations but one choice. It was to make itself some latter-day version of the Spanish Republic or turn right as it made its way out of the decades of dictatorship. The decisive figures were Álvaro Cunhal, the stoically charismatic leader of the PCP, the Portuguese Communist Party, and Mario Soáres, whose Socialists were much given to accredited membership in the Western alliance. It was not difficult to discern the Cold War as it arrived, or to see it in the American press coverage of these events.

The PCP's prominence at the time cannot be overstated, though it is important to understand what it was and was not. Having endured clandestinely for decades, it emerged in 1974 a disciplined "wall of steel," as members and supporters described it. The party was everywhere, the work of many underground comrades over many years. I laughed aloud when, during a weekend by the ocean south of Lisbon, I spotted PCP beach balls and umbrellas in the party's red and yellow colors. It was especially strong in Alentejo, the broad, flat region southeast of Lisbon, where peasants lived in poor villages next to large *latifundia* whose absentee owners used them to hunt once or twice a year. On an estate villagers had taken over, one of many, earnest teenagers tilled hectares of tomatoes and beans with translations of

Marx in their back pockets. At the edge of a field, a recently arrived Soviet tractor glinted in the sun.

Cunhal appeared the very picture of a Stalinist strongman. Lean, silver-haired, handsome in the chiseled-features way, he had a lot of prison time on his face by the time he took the PCP above ground in 1974. Contrary to the clichéd caricatures in the Western press, I detected a subtle but palpable humanity behind the taciturn demeanor. His loyalty to Moscow lay beyond question, but this was a remnant of his younger years, as I read it, and the sentiment of a figure who had never held power. Eurocommunist leaders were then emerging in Spain, France, and Italy—three Latin nations, or in France's case partly Latin. In my estimation, Cunhal would have taken his place among them had the formidable apparatus behind him carried the PCP to power.

The Portugal I saw and reported was struggling to become a nation of its own making—neither Moscow's nor Washington's. Its people had come through the revolution with uplifted eyes, their legible preferences running to nonalignment and one or another kind of social democracy. But this was not to be. The political impasse seemed to invite a covert CIA operation, and the agency accepted as was its well-established wont. Firsthand now, I watched as Washington made another nation one of its experiments in altered reality and as the American press played POLO with abandon.

Reports of the CIA's presence began to see print within a few months of the 25th April revolution. The newly enlivened Lisbon dailies were dense with such stories. That autumn, 1974, The Associated Press reported that the agency had a hundred operatives on the ground. We now know the Ford administration fully intended to intervene to block a NATO member's leftward drift. The question was how to get this done.

Henry Kissinger, then Ford's secretary of state, favored an alliance with extreme-right political parties and a military intervention—effectively a repeat of the Chilean coup two years earlier. Frank Carlucci, the new ambassador to Lisbon, argued for a covert political operation aimed at the opportunist middle—those to the right of the PCP but to the left of the arch-conservative parties. Carlucci won Kissinger over, and his strategy, when realized, bore striking resemblance to the

CIA's subversion of Italy's elections in behalf of Christian Democrats in 1948 (and for many years afterward).

Carlucci was no stranger to clandestine interventions. Within days of his arrival in January 1975, he settled on Soáres, identified by this time as a political main-chancer, as the principal channel through which he would manage his operation. This amounted to a money-funneling scheme focused on ranking army officers, center-right and center-left political parties, the press, and some elements in the highly influential Catholic Church. Carlucci's operation was covert only in its finer details. It was prima facie plain since his appointment, which was front-page news in Lisbon, that Washington had made Portugal another of its Cold War theaters. The Portuguese were incensed by this intrusion into their post-revolutionary affairs. Demonstrations in front of the American Embassy and Carlucci's residence were so frequent the government—reluctantly at first—sent troops to protect them. Things nonetheless went Washington's way soon enough. Soáres took office as premier six months after the hot summer drew to a close.

These events, by way of declassified documents, scholarly research, interviews, and oral histories, are now a matter of record. What struck me as I covered them was how aware Portuguese were of what was unfolding around them and how plainly they were able to speak and write of it. It was like listening to a new political language—clear, to the point, no cotton wool to it. Americans—and how could I fail to notice?—read nothing of Washington's machinations in Lisbon, nothing of Carlucci's intervention. I was face to face with the ideological contaminations of American correspondents abroad. I found *The New York Times* coverage especially dishonest by way of its fractionally accurate reports and frequent omissions, notably those concerning Carlucci's operation, the realities of which were perfectly available to anyone with open eyes and ears. *The Times* made full use of the contingent nature of Arendt's fragile, isolated facts. This was brazen malpractice—my estimation then and now.

I took instruction in these and other such matters during my time in Portugal. All correspondents bring their politics with them—a natural thing, a good thing, an affirmation of their engaged, civic selves not at all to be regretted. The task is to manage your politics in accord with your professional responsibilities, the unique place correspondents occupy in public space. There could be no confusing journalism and activism, as I had seen on West Seventeenth Street. While we commonly associate this error with independent publications, let us be clear: Every mainstream journalist serving the national security state is guilty of it—every one an activist. It requires discipline and ordered priorities to get this question right. Learning these was a project of mine at this early moment in my professional life. I count this point as important now as I did then.

I had also learned by this time to dispose of the Manichean Cold War prejudices drilled into every American born at midcentury or later—another lesson I have ever since valued. A tractor donated as foreign aid needn't be understood as anything more than a tractor unless there is evidence otherwise, in the way a cigar is more often than not just a cigar. It was a correspondent's place to report as truthfully as he or she could on the doings of others, whether or not one approved. Marvine Howe, *The Times*'s gritty, seasoned correspondent in Lisbon at the time and long controversial for her proximity to the powers she reported on when these powers were conservative, would have rung the "Red menace" bell loudly had she set eyes on that tractor in Alentejo. Marvine was an activist. During the *verão quente* and the crucial months that followed, I will add, it was widely understood among other correspondents that she was—how to put it?—inappropriately close to Soáres as he collaborated with Carlucci. One was not altogether surprised.

Portugal was formative to the beginner I was then. It was a first attempt to report and write as the correspondent I aspired to be—filing to an independent press, holding to professional standards others around me had vacated. In the personal terms I choose, for a brief time my shadow and I were one, integrated and whole. As I made my way home, a thousand lessons crammed into a Portuguese army backpack I picked up in a surplus shop, I knew I was about to learn another: I would see more clearly than ever the darkness within which the American press confined American readers.

I paused in Toulouse en route back to Paris for my flight home. A kindly Toulousain of a certain age took me to see the large fields outside the city where Spanish refugees had taken shelter after fleeing the Franco regime forty years earlier. Half a million Spaniards had fled to grim, improvised camps on the French side of the Pyrénées and along the Atlantic coast. This was called *la Retirada*, the Retreat. It was my first glimpse, in its early stage, of the ideological confrontation that marked the twentieth century. In those fields—ghostly fields, as the old man told of them, haunted fields—I saw in the mind's eye the human cost of it. For many of those refugees there was no going back. I thought of my journey to Lisbon, of how the train from Paris was filled with Portuguese maids and manual laborers the dictatorship had dispossessed. Would they have a country of their own now?

How many American correspondents would even understand such a question? Martha Gellhorn once described journalism as an honorable exchange between reporter and reader. Where lay the honor now? How many correspondents knew even to ask?

BACK IN NEW YORK, I discovered Jack Smith had published very few of the files I had sent by post. I had reported the campaigns against the Gonçalves government, the splinter parties that had sprouted after the revolution, the American Embassy's intrigues, what I saw in the countryside. But alas, all I had learned and absorbed notwithstanding, I simply hadn't gotten all the way to finding my feet as a correspondent. In the main, I had failed to situate myself properly between the events I was covering and my readers: I was too close to the former and too distant from the latter. Getting this right is something every correspondent has to learn, and there is no learning it other than in the field. The unused files mattered to me, but not overmuch. It was the doing of it that counted. Getting spiked, in any case, is an experience correspondents are best off having early.

Jack had especially liked a report I sent from Braga, a notoriously right-wing provincial city in Portugal's rural northwest. I had driven up with Dutch friends to hear the fire-breathing Eduardo Melo Peixoto, the canon of Braga, deliver a speech that was the talk of Lisbon in the days preceding it. Melo was a richly robed fanatic straight out of the Catholic-Fascist movement of the Salazar years, and he brought the packed square outside the fifteenth-century cathedral and along the streets leading to it to a boiling frenzy against the provisional government. Jack liked the on-the-ground tactility I put into the file—the "actuality," as radio people call it. I learned a lesson that day, another that has never left me: There is no judging or reporting the course of a revolution without reference to the counterrevolution it inevitably prompts. And yet another lesson atop that one: Rarely will the mainstream dailies provide this essential context. None, to my knowledge, sent a correspondent to cover Melo, a key figure among the reactionary coup-plotters and known to have connections to terror groups responsible for numerous right-wing bomb attacks during those tumultuous months.

In a short while Jack named me foreign editor, taking over a desk vacated while I was away. I took to the task with alacrity, giving Jack weekly foreign reports as strong as any the paper had ever run, so far as I could make out as I wandered among the archives. There was excellent material from Angola and the other nations now free of Portuguese rule. Our coverage of southern Africa and Southeast Asia was nonpareil among independent publications. We stayed on top of the Eurocommunism phenomenon.

Pieces arrived by post from one Christopher Knowles, among the numerous correspondents I inherited. Knowles filed from Argentina, where American-backed army colonels were "disappearing" leftists of all stripes and democrats of even the mildest sort. He eventually stopped filing, sending no further word. Months later I drew close to a new neighbor on the Upper West Side called Paul Hoeffel. Soon enough it emerged that Paul was my Christopher Knowles. He and his partner, an accomplished Latin Americanist named Judith Evans, had fled via a flight to Spain hours before the military junta's death squads arrived at their Buenos Aires apartment in their telltale Ford Falcons.

My reconnection with Wilfred mattered much to me. I was his editor now, but for when Jack assumed this duty. Some of his files arrived via post on onionskin paper from Paris, from Luanda, from Lourenço Marques. There was more dictation. I came to savor his diction, the unabashed clarity of his language. "The my-juh Wes-tin pahz" was a favorite: simple, no cotton wool to it, a phrase the mainstream dailies never used in referring to the Western alliance for precisely these attributes.

When Cedric Belfrage and Jim Aronson resigned years earlier, Wilfred had at first concluded he ought to go with them. He determined to keep filing, thankfully from my perspective, because he thought Americans should see his work. But the ideological Pharisees repelled him as much as they did Cedric, Jim Aronson, me, and others. A great deal of mud had been flung in Wilfred's direction over the years—"agent of influence," KGB operative, traitor to the West, and so forth—but the man I heard on the telephone and whose letters I opened was first and last a correspondent. In the course of forty years, he had filed for *The Times* of London, the *Daily Express*, and other such publications—experience that showed. Harrison Salisbury, who possessed one of the few independent minds among *The New York Times*'s faux-august grandees, later wrote the introduction to *At the Barricades*, Wilfred's memoirs. The Depression had left a mark on him and the Cold War another, Salisbury accurately observed. It and the liberation struggles the Cold War so often complicated were ever after his true subjects. "He never quite cut his connections with conventional newspapering," Salisbury noted, also accurately. "In many ways Burchett reminds one more of the old-fashioned pre-1917 radicals than those of today's highly ideological confrontations, a Lincoln Steffens or a John Reed with an Australian accent." This was a good thumbnail of the man I edited.

I met Wilfred only once, when he was in New York and the *Guardian* arranged for him to speak in a school auditorium somewhere off Irving Place. He made his distaste for the paper's direction pointedly plain. This pleased me. Jack and the other senior editors listened in silence, and this pleased me, too. Wilfred was of his time, and I would be of mine. I would be my own kind of correspondent. But this encounter was reassuring: I wasn't as alone as I often felt in the Seventeenth Street loft.

The wheel turned in time. What went on around me came to seem a reënactment of the same purification rituals one found in the McCarthy obsessions—a perverse mirror. I gave Jack a professionally edited foreign report every week, but the very poor standard of journalism I so often found around me crept up on me. I saw the connection between the disciplines I had learned at the *Daily News*, and that Wilfred brought to the paper, and any publication's credibility. The medium bore part of the message, I had to conclude. There seemed no further point in associating with a paper in the once-was-but-no-longer category. Not long after I resigned, I should add, so did Wilfred. He quit in 1980, as disgusted as Belfrage with "ideological virgins."

Many years later and by the unlikeliest of circumstances, I was introduced to George Burchett, one of Wilfred's sons. He was living, and still lives, in Hanoi, his birthplace, and is a very fine painter. We made extraordinary discoveries across the decades. George was in his early twenties when I was editing Wilfred, and he sometimes listened to his father read me his pieces from Meudon. "There are two sounds I remember very fondly," he wrote in a touching letter. "The sound of his electric Smith-Corona in the morning—he usually started around 4 a.m. The sound of his voice dictating his weekly *Guardian* story. Both sounds meant DAD WAS HOME."

I cannot do better than to quote from a note I sent George about his father at the time:

He was a kind of ideal to the twenty-five-year-old I describe. I admired his professionalism and his commitment to applying this to a journalism he believed in. He made me recognize that the independent press as it was then had too few, if any, like him. W/o meaning to, Wilfred helped me set my own path. I made up my mind to put in my years with the mainstream press, acquire experience and craft, and by the time I was done w/ this, far in the future, there would be a vibrant, sustaining alternative to the mainstream. So one could think back then, Saigon having risen.

I regret neither my years at the *Guardian* nor leaving it when the time came. What I learned in Portugal and while serving as foreign editor has never left me. I knew the world a lot better by the time I was done. And good enough that I acquired an education in the literature of revolution. Lenin's coldly analytic mind was nothing if not disciplined. Reading Marx taught me the worth of intellectual structure—how to frame events in history, think in the terms of political economy, and identify interests, especially class interests when they are pertinent (as they nearly always are). These habits of mind—rare among correspondents, I have found—have ever since served me in good stead.

But I no more belonged on West Seventeenth Street, given what was becoming of the paper whose heritage I so admired, than I had on East Forty-Second. They were varieties of alienation, both made of people who saw what they wished to see. My grail still awaited finding.

# 2.

# The Ill-Fitting Suits of the Soviets.

> The foreigner is within me, hence
> we are all foreigners. If I am a
> foreigner, there are no foreigners.
>
> ——Julia Kristeva,
> *Strangers to Ourselves,*
> 1991.

M Y *GUARDIAN* WAGE had been ninety dollars a week, handed out Fridays in the small manila envelopes the English call "pay packets." Suddenly I was down to unemployment checks. I recall sitting in my apartment one early-autumn afternoon, watching tugboats navigate barges on the Hudson, savings book in hand: I had three hundred sixty-five dollars and counted it enough. The vast world beyond the river seemed to lie benignly before me. Where, when young, do some of us find within ourselves such sweet certainty?

Work was easier to come by then, and I shortly bluffed my way onto the staff at *Business Week*, of all places. *BW*, where the disciplines were rigorous, drilled a lot of craft into me over the next several years. The *Financial Times*, at this time timidly crossing the Atlantic, eventually invited me to London—someone to lend American idiom to the endeavor. So began a year among the English. I fell in with a spirited group publishing a political monthly called *The Leveller*, named after the radical democrats of the English Civil War, while doing a little stringing for the *Guardian* as occasions arose. Writing on the side for other-than-mainstream newspapers and journals, often using *noms de plume*, became a practice I kept up for many years.

One afternoon the telephone rang at Bracken House, the *FT*'s building in the City. I was out to lunch, and the message left on my desk read, "Allan Siegel, 212. 556. 1234." I recognized the number and knew Siegel by name: He was news editor at *The New York Times*. Was I interested in joining the editing staff, he asked when I returned his call. By this time I also knew *The Times*'s reputation as the most unpleasant newsroom in the trade. With gnashing teeth, I accepted when I returned to New York as the nineteen seventies tipped into the eighties.

My misgivings were well-founded. The West Forty-Third Street newsroom (in the old *Times* building) turned out to be worse than my worst imaginings. Ill will and bloody-mindedness were ground into the worn industrial carpet. There was too much power at stake—my diagnosis—and too many people pursuing it too single-mindedly. Editors and reporters seemed to think solely of appearing clever "out front," where the managing editors sat. I could detect only slight interest in what was going on in the world and into the news pages. No wonder so many journalists, forgetting why they were journalists, were indifferent to or simply unaware of their place in the ideological order. Getting in, getting wise, and getting out never seemed so fine an idea.

I had learned in Lisbon years earlier that there was no understanding the Captains' Coup without a grasp of the African colonies. It was the senseless inhumanity of the Portuguese as the empire decayed that had inspired the Armed Forces Movement to revolt. Africa, Central and Southern, became an abiding interest, and this began to set my path. On my return from Portugal I had begun part-time graduate work in African history at Columbia under the guidance of a distinguished Africanist named Marcia Wright. Lisbon and the M.A. work drew me toward the developing world—its problems, the countless up-from-the-bottom tasks such nations faced, above all the aspirations one saw across what was by this time called the South. I began writing from the United Nations for various third-world journals, some in English, some in French. Among these was a monthly called *Southern Africa*, published by South African exiles living, as I was, on Manhattan's Upper West Side. Most of these publications reside now in archives. But another door opened, this one giving onto the West's great Other.

During these years I also served as a special correspondent—a stringer, a freelancer—attached to the New York bureau of *The Economist*. Whenever I went to Rockefeller Center, where the bureau was located, I would stop at the entrance of The Associated Press Building, at 50 Rock, and look up at Isamu Noguchi's *News*, the celebrated bas-relief he installed in 1940. The dynamism of the piece—the kinetic energy and urgency Noguchi inscribed in his stainless-steel figures—never failed to draw me into it. I allowed myself to think I shared a common purpose with his reporters, his photographer, and his rewrite man. And, were I among them above The A.P.'s front door, I would insist that the work of independent journalists, all of it, mattered as much as anything that went on inside the building. I could not then have put it in these terms, but I wanted to think Noguchi's figures were at one with their shadows.

I was not on the foreign desk at *The Times*, but I followed the coverage with an eye for the well done and the other than. What I saw left me as cold as the animus that suffused the newsroom. Correspondents are, or ought to be, in the business of representation—or re-presentation, better put. They are their readers' eyes on the world. They evoke and stabilize realities few readers will ever see for themselves. This leaves correspondents with an immense responsibility. Wide-open eyes and ears, an intent gaze, a determination to keep the coverage as clear as possible of politics and ideology: These are essential to good work. There were some fine correspondents in the field when I joined *The Times*—fine as technicians, this is to say. In the ethos of *The Times*, a good correspondent was one who could parachute into an unfamiliar country and file a sound story within twenty-four hours. This amounted to a cult of superficiality and was not without its ideological implications. Most *Times* correspondents took pride in measuring up to this standard. But as they defined and fixed their readers' relations with the world, most of them did not bear well the responsibility I describe.

The essential conveyance I found in *The Times*'s daily foreign report was the supposed reality of difference, the making and maintaining of a psychological construct commonly called "Self and Other." Any people *Times* correspondents covered—and this judgment is by no means limited to them—might be friendly or hostile, familiar or "inscrutable" (that ever-freighted term), but they were always different,

always not like us, always Other. This seemed to me the irreducible
wrong in the way the American press covered the world. It was partly
a consequence of Cold War ideology and partly the perspective of
what was by this time an imperium gazing over its dominion. But
the question ran deeper. What I read was most fundamentally a daily
affirmation of American exceptionalism: There were we God-gifted
Americans, and there were the other-than-exceptional "they" of the
world. Correspondents were not so much opening Americans' eyes as
purporting to open them while keeping them wide shut.

*The Times*, to put the point another way, was where I witnessed
the culture of ignorance I have already mentioned as it was day-to-
day produced and reproduced. To betray this culture, to write truly of
other people as they were and thought and felt and saw the world, was
to "go native"—a not-unserious transgression. A few correspondents
crossed this line from time to time. This typically prompted the foreign editor either to send them elsewhere in the bureau network or to
pull them back for duty in the Trenton bureau or some other inglorious
place. This is why bureau rotation, a standard tour lasting three to five
years, was a common practice at the time. Don't wade too far into
the country you're covering, stay on our side of the pane of glass that
separates us from them, and observe the law of superficiality: These
were the unwritten rules. Bureau rotation is less common now because
it is expensive and—my surmise—because recent cohorts of correspondents are sufficiently indoctrinated that straying beyond the fence
posts of Self and Other never occurs to them. As I consider the *Times*
correspondents now in the field I can think of no exception.

I saw no future at *The Times*. I had reported Portugal as a
correspondent, not as an American correspondent. I had carried no
template in my shoulder bag, no ideological die. Taking a lesson from
Wilfred Burchett—one of his most essential—I had made it a point to
live and move among the people of whom I was writing. I have ever
since worked according to a commitment I made then: Nothing is too
complex for the general reader so long as one takes the time, and it
may be a lot of time, to write clearly in language one has learned to
control. Neither before nor since have I had any time for the cult of
the superficial.

But Portugal was behind me, and *The Times* took only passing
interest in developing nations, the North-South divide, and numerous

other questions I thought worth a correspondent's while. It left too much of the world out. One day a friend telephoned with a suggestion. Bob Manning and I had often covered the U.N. together for *Jeune Afrique, African Development, Afrique-Asie*, and other such journals, and he understood how miserable I was on West Forty-Third Street. Bob knew the scene (though to my abiding chagrin he later went over to our kindly friends in Langley). "You should write a letter to the *Far Eastern Economic Review*," he advised when he called that snowy winter evening. "Here's the managing editor's name."

I knew the magazine. The *Fareer*, as it was sometimes called back then, had an excellent and pleasingly eccentric reputation. It was a writer's publication, not an editor's—a considerable mark in its favor. I wrote the letter.

HERE AND THERE IN THE NOVELS, Conrad remarks that one could detect the smells of the East when still a couple of days out from landfall—"the first sigh of the East," as he writes of its odors in *Youth.* I have long assumed he wanted to capture the strangeness Westerners felt when drawing near the islands and harbors he had so long sailed among. The thought came again as I made my way along the Hong Kong waterfront to the *Review's* offices on Gloucester Road. These were my first steps in Asia. Amid the din of grinding diesel buses, honking taxis, and shouting Cantonese shopkeepers, there were the odors I would know for many years—dried fish, roasted ducks hung in windows, worn wooden bins of rice, gunny sacks of woven jute filled with herbal medicines, mushrooms, tea, spices, Tianjin peppers, vegetables I had never before seen. And there at the seaside edge of Wanchai, still the world of many Suzie Wongs, the last of the British crown colony's open sewers. Strange smells that day, they were in time familiar, the odors of the Other until I understood that I was the Other and at last that there was no Other and that the color of one's skin or the shape of one's eyes had nothing to do with who one was.

When I walked into the *Review's* cramped editorial offices, a crusty copy editor named Richard Breeze looked up and missed no beat. "You're the new American," he growled in a voice his Gitanes habit had turned to gravel. "Your president's just been shot." This puts the start of what turned out to be long, life-altering years at 30 March 1981. I now read more into that greeting than I did at the time. The *Review* teemed with nationalities—British, Australians, Canadians, Chinese, Indians, Singaporeans, Malaysians, numerous others—and I was not the only American. But there was in *Review* culture, at bottom English newspaper culture, a not-altogether-subtle disapproval of the nation that carried too big a stick in Asia and had too lively a givenness to guns. I have just named two of the magazine's great strengths: an unusually diverse staff and a wary eye toward American power.

Edited and published in Hong Kong, the *Review* had no nation whose perspective it was obliged to reflect. Neither did it have a publisher or an ownership structure setting any kind of ideological course. Hongkong and Shanghai Bank, *grande dame* of Western financial institutions in the East since the eighteen eighties, had a controlling share in the magazine and left it to its own devices. "Unique" is a term journalists were once trained to use cautiously—what under the sun is unique?—but in these respects the *Review* came close. You remained an Indonesian or an Indian or an American, but you didn't report as one. I didn't have to wear the tight shoes Western newspapers, magazines, and broadcasters required their correspondents to walk in as a matter of course.

Derek Davies, the *Review*'s longtime editor, was a singular man by any reckoning. Welsh by background, he had served as a British diplomat but resigned when he married Shizue Sanada, a Japanese—this considered a security risk at the time. When Derek took the editor's chair in 1965, the *Review* had a staff of five and was a few pages printed on telephone-book paper. By the time I arrived it had a lively newsroom, nine bureaus ("bureaux," as the idiosyncratic Derek insisted the masthead designate them), and a circulation of seventy-five thousand. The cheap paper remained, making *Review* photographs famously muddy. But those of power and influence in Asia—diplomats, cabinet ministers, MPs, opposition pols, barristers and judges, scholars, bankers, investors, commodity traders—could not afford to miss the *Review* when it came out each Thursday. In a region where a free press was not much more than a pretense, it had authority deriving from its authenticity. My irreducible definition of journalism is "seeing and saying." *Review* correspondents saw and said.

Derek, it is time to note, had been MI6 during his years at the Foreign Office, serving at one point in Saigon. If his view of America and Americans was ambivalent, his view of the Cold War wasn't. But a *Review* correspondent carried neither a spear nor water for Washington. All of us, not least Derek, had too much respect for Asia and Asians. There was no reporting of either as anyone's Other and certainly no assigning anyone bit parts in America's long-running John Ford Western. This was the greatest of the *Review*'s editorial strengths and what distinguished it in the English-language press. Out of many nationalities, it had no nationality. *E pluribus nullus.*

There were some noted names on the masthead by the time I arrived in Hong Kong. Nayan Chanda, the well-connected diplomatic correspondent, was read the world over for his insider's reporting on Indochina. David Bonavia, a former *Times* of London correspondent, filed the most nuanced copy coming out of Beijing at the time. No one dissected the mainland's political economy, then in profound transformation, with the detail and subtlety Robert Delfs brought to his assignment. Ho Kwon Ping, as economics correspondent, wrote with unmatched insight on North-South questions: third-world debt, the ruinous policies of the multilateral institutions, the various development strategies then in fashion. It was when Kwon Ping resigned to take a place in his family business in Singapore—an honorable gesture of filial piety but a swerve in his trajectory—that I was invited to replace him. I was to fill a very large pair of *yun peng* slippers.

As it happened, I had little time even to attempt the high intellectual ground Kwon Ping had left to me. Staff changes—a reassignment from Singapore, a resignation in Kuala Lumpur—left empty bureaus, and I began shuttling between these two cities within a couple of months of my arrival. Malaysia and Lee Kuan Yew's authoritarian city-state were our most important circulation centers for reasons just suggested: You read the *Straits Times* (Singapore) and the *New Straits Times* (Kuala Lumpur) for the official versions of events; you read the *Review* for an accurate accounting. I ran up and down the Malay Peninsula for months. It was a forty-five-minute flight between Singapore and K.L. The editing desk at the *New York Times* was an aeon away as I plunged headfirst into places, populations, and histories I had no choice but to learn as quickly as I could, a dancer sent on stage without rehearsal.

Malaysia was a reliably lively scene whenever I arrived—rich in resources, politically argumentative, corrupt to the tops of its oil palms. Its prime minister at this time, Mahathir bin Mohamad, bore a *ressentiment* toward the West I found interesting, provocative, and ever a source of good copy. Malaysia's politics were defined by contending populations—the wealthy *huaqiao* (Overseas Chinese), the Malay majority, whose culture derived from the *kampong*, the thatch-roofed village, and an articulate minority of Indians whose ancestors the British had shipped across the Andaman Sea to tap rubber, mine tin, and harvest palm oil.

K.L. was a joy to report in those days. The ambition that gave it its kinetic character took place in a city in some ways not much changed from "the British time," as Indian friends put it. My morning walk to the bureau led through meadows of knee-high grass and wandering chickens—the *kampong* in the capital. I took my sundowners with the city's intellectuals and dissidents at a colonial-era bar called the Coliseum Café, once a resting place for planters when they came to the colonial capital for supplies. In a hotel bookshop I came upon a collection of essays called *Malaysia 2000*. In it a group of economists offered their thoughts as to where the nation would find itself two decades out. One of them held there was no understanding a place unless you spent long hours walking around in it. I had already made this method mine. I found a vibrantly awakened nation, but there was something amiss in its nervous energy—something not settled, something unagreed-upon. Its forward movement seemed made as much of anxiety and longing as of purpose.

I reported all this just as I saw it. My closest press colleagues—from *The Times* of London, the *FT*, the BBC, *Le Monde*, ANSA, the Italian wire service—were infrequent travelers on the shuttle and took but passing interest in matters not of direct concern in London or Paris or Rome. They kept their bureaus in Singapore and found it conveniently serviceable as they covered the entire region. In Singapore, the telephones worked (not always the case in Kuala Lumpur and elsewhere), it was clean (certainly not always the case), and efficient (most certainly not). Colleagues understood Singapore as well as I did, if not better. Behind the veneer of a Westminster democracy—seventy-five MPs in a unicameral legislature, judges in robes and English perukes—it was a stifling, psychologically injurious police state intolerant of the faintest whisper of dissent. How many humane souls, excellently educated and knowing right from wrong, cut themselves in two, letting their civic selves wither while they got on with their private lives and the making of their fortunes? Colleagues rarely reported "the island republic," as we inevitably called the place on second mention. On those occasions they did, their stories didn't circulate locally; mine did, a source of considerable peril as I was soon to discover. Were Singapore in Eastern Europe, Western correspondents would have reported it as a repressive Soviet satellite. Under the Southeast Asian sun, it was put across as "the garden city" and other such contrivances. My sin, when I committed it, was in refusing to traffic in this Cold War imagery.

M Y BIVOUAC WHEN in Singapore during those early months was a fusty suite overlooking the courtyard at Raffles, the once-grand hotel not far from the Singapore Cricket Club and the banks of the befouled Singapura River. Local friends, especially the young, didn't care for the place, and I took a lesson from their courteous foot-shuffling whenever I suggested we gather there. Newly arrived Westerners are commonly fascinated by these evocative colonial artifacts. Raffles was another monument to the unconscious Orientalism still evident in the years of which I write. In time it reminded me that somewhere beneath their natural graciousness, many Asians nursed a variant of that old *ressentiment* toward the West I detected in Mahathir, the Malaysian prime minister. Most Westerners, and I include most Western correspondents, miss this. I lived amid a world passing and another arriving. If I were fortunate, the same passage would occur within me, and I would think of all "exotic fables of the East," Somerset Maugham's phrase, as those around me thought of them—of another time, not to be inhabited.

One evening, just back from Kuala Lumpur, I sat in the Long Bar at Raffles perusing the local dailies, opening mail, and reading telexes. There were a few lines from Guy Sacerdoti, the *Review's* bureau chief in Jakarta. Could we talk?

I put a call through the next morning. At this point, in the early 1980s, the South China Sea and the Gulf of Thailand were dense with Vietnamese "boat people" hoping to make landfall somewhere in

Southeast Asia and then resettle in Canada, America, France, or else-where in the West. The Western press put this crisis down to Hanoi's cruelties. One read of reëducation camps, forced resettlements, purges, postwar revenge—the full-dress horror show when the Western dailies and wires reported on Eastern bloc nations. Hanoi was forcing its people into the sea, as the Cold War narrative had it.

"That doesn't seem to be the story," Guy said. The line was crackly, as it often was on Jakarta calls. He described a stifled mutiny among refugee officials around the region, who charged that Western propaganda was enticing Vietnamese into dangerous journeys as part of Washington's "bleed Vietnam white" policy—its campaign to deplete the nation of as many productive people as it could. Guy mentioned the Vietnamese-language broadcasts the Voice of America and the BBC beamed nightly into Vietnamese cities, towns, and villages. "Nobody's pushing anyone into the South China Sea, from what I'm hearing," Guy said. "This looks like a crisis created in Washington. It's pull, not push."

"Let's do it," I said immediately. The U.N.'s regional refugee office was three flights down from the *Review* bureau. I could cover the Pulau Bidong camp, population twelve thousand, off Malaysia's east coast. There was another large camp on Pulau Galang, an otherwise uninhabited Indonesian island a few miles beyond Singaporean waters.

"No, man. I'm too busy," Guy replied. "It's your banana."

I peeled the banana and found the expected rot within. In the camps I met a people more dignified than any I had known. I saw the self-possession of those who had endured the B-52s and the napalm to defeat the world's most powerful military. But I had to set aside admiration and the stirred heart to understand what I saw. Those fleeing political persecution—collaborators with the Americans or the Saigon government, chiefly—were refugees by the accepted definition and had long since found their way Westward. Those I was meeting, their native poise aside, were economic migrants enticed by American dreams dangled before them. Some of the young men were simply avoiding military service.

I gave the story arduous weeks. Up to eighty percent of those in the camps were either straight-out opportunists or draft dodgers, to put the point plainly. The American officials I met were bitter. Washington was either suppressing their field reports, classifying them, rewriting them, ignoring them, or removing those who wrote them. A propaganda operation seemed evident. Congress was approving resettlement quotas for refugees who did not even exist. These numbers, featured regularly on those VOA and BBC programs, were provocations. The "Saigon cowboys" at the State Department—those with long experience in Indochina, many with Vietnamese wives—had for years advanced the refugee program as an American obligation, a matter of compassion. I returned to Hong Kong with a satchel of interview notes and documents showing this to be a contemptible ruse, dutifully reproduced in the American press.

It took hand-wringing days to get the piece down as I wanted it. Derek quickly determined it was a cover story. Letters arrived in the weeks after we published "Refugees: The Pull Factor," as the cover language read. The BBC denied any such broadcasting campaign as I had described. The State Department sent a lengthy complaint that didn't directly refute anything we had published. With a colleague's generous assist, I had come upon a campaign to destabilize a nation America still considered an adversary while scoring a disinformation victory of transcendent cynicism, given the cavalier use it made of nearly a million lives. This was my second direct exposure, after mid-seventies Portugal, to an American intervention as it unfolded— one way the Cold War was waged in Asia for a time after the 1975 defeat. And one way among many it was badly reported.

D EREK USED TO CALL Donald Wise "the David Niven of journalism." Donald was a ringer for the British actor and shared with Niven that debonair, grace-under-fire dash the Edwardian English excelled at projecting. He had an eventful career as a British officer and a war correspondent before he arrived at the *Review* a few years before I did. Captured in Singapore when the colony fell to the Japanese in early 1942, he was among those force-marched up the Malay Peninsula to Burma to build the famous River Kwai bridge. I dislike the word "legendary," hyperbolic in almost all cases, but if one insisted, it suited Donald better than most. Around the office he was "Unca Donald."

One day he waved me over to his desk and told me there was someone he wanted me to meet. I was fresh from my refugee exposé and coasting for a few days. I figured Donald thought his friend or contact—I couldn't make this out—would be someone it would serve me to know, a useful source.

"How would next Tuesday be? Lunch."

"I should be clear," I replied.

"Here's the address. Lockhart Road. One o'clock. Splendid tuck."

The man I was to meet was with Chemical Bank, prominent then, since long gone. He served as a regional political analyst or some such indeterminate title.

Along I went. It was a crowded, dish-clattering Vietnamese place in Wanchai where the food was indeed excellent. Here I must be honest. Our sea scallops, pork, and bok choy were nearly gone before it hit me that my host wanted more of me than he had on offer. All his casually posed questions suddenly seemed to have a point. The man from Chemical was English. This was an MI6 vetting. By way of Robert Delfs, my colleague on the China side, I have since come by considerable detail of my host's career as an intelligence operative: He served undercover behind Japanese lines during World War II, then held MI6 posts in K.L., Hanoi, Ulan Bator, and, as station chief, Washington.

Nothing came of this encounter. One way or another I hadn't measured up. I recall my lunch companion's name but will not use it. As we finished he said with English courtesy, "If you wouldn't mind, best not to mention we've met or that I'm with Chemical. The bank prefers it this way."

The bank prefers it.

Derek had been MI6 as a matter of record, though we all assumed he wasn't active during his *Review* decades. Neither was there cause to think Unca Donald was more than a fellow traveler in a mirror image of the term's meaning. You came across this sort of thing everywhere you turned among journalists serving overseas during these years. That lunch seemed to me, then as now, a favor on Donald's part of the sort that helped keep the old Wurlitzer running. Now I knew firsthand the music of it, the etiquette of the exercise. And that what I had read of years earlier was still accepted procedure. I've since had ample reasons to conclude with certainty it remains so.

THE SOVIETS HAD their Cold War satellites. Poland, East Germany, Czechoslovakia, Hungary, the others. These were unfree nations where silence prevailed in the public square, where all orders emanated from Moscow, where culture was forced underground and literature mimeographed. Western correspondents were expected to file the grimmest possible reports, no boilerplate too overworked. Who does not recall the *LIFE* magazine spreads wherein the paint always peeled in the rail stations and there was one desiccated head of cabbage on the produce shelf? My favorite of the Cold War decades' many banalities had to do with Soviet and East European tailoring. I wish I could count the news reports wherein some high official appeared before Western correspondents "in an ill-fitting suit." Maybe some readers will remember this foolishness; it was a favorite at *The Times*. "Mr. Ponomarev, who appeared wearing an ill-fitting suit, stated Moscow's objections to the new NATO exercises." So it would be told. Anything to remind us of the inferiority of the Other and the otherness of the inferior. To my delight, *The Times* still trots out this silly cliché from time to time. As I wrote this chapter its Moscow correspondent informed us that Aleksandr Lukashenko, the president of Belarus and among Washington's current crop of adversaries, makes his way around Minsk in ill-fitting suits.

The Cold War imagery was very different in East Asia, where the satellites were ours. There was not an ill-fitting suit to be found. From Korea south through Indonesia, economies thrived by the mid–Cold War years—"miracles," as Americans were urged to think of them. Except that there were no miracles at the western end of the Pacific. Asia's new prosperity was in large measure the consequence of Washington's Cold War counter to the socialist alternative. It induced a remarkable run of economic dynamism, in part by making America the primary market for the region's exports: T-shirts, transistor radios, and plastic toys at first, later on machine tools, cars, computers, steel, high-end medical equipment. America's constellation of satellites was never so named, but there was no denying this is what East Asian nations conscripted to the Cold War cause were. Once you looked honestly at these nations, it was easy to see that East Asians shared much with the Poles and Czechs. Their leaders obeyed Washington on all matters of consequence; public life was blighted, cultures were emaciated, genuine democracy was not on offer, and there was the same danger attaching to dissent.

At the core of the region's political economy lay what I came to call "the Cold War social contract." This entailed a rigorously enforced exchange between the governing and the governed—or rulers and ruled, better put. Those in power assured their citizens a measure of material prosperity. Refrigerators, televisions, washing machines, and air conditioners arrived in many Asian households for the first time. In exchange, the citizenry had to surrender its voice in all political matters. Power sequestered itself, the political process became mere spectacle, and citizens became consumers (just as they had in Cold War America). As a thumbnail explanatory I took to summarizing this arrangement as "Shut up and change the channel." The Western press uniformly left unreported this essential feature of life as it was in Asia. But the *Review* was not, as noted, altogether a Western publication.

Some months after my encounter with the MI6 man, Derek suggested lunch at the Foreign Correspondents' Club. Philip Bowring, deputy editor at this time and the man who had brought me out from New York, joined us. Would I like to take over in Singapore, where they hadn't yet replaced the transferred bureau chief? I accepted, my misgivings about the sterility of Lee Kuan Yew's shop-window republic notwithstanding.

Lee's city-state was about to get interesting. A couple of weeks earlier, a working-class district called Anson had elected Singapore's first opposition MP in nearly twenty years. Even the winning candidate, a fifty-five-year-old barrister named J.B. Jeyaretnam, was stunned. The ruling People's Action Party fell into a frenetic panic. The PAP was organized on Leninist lines—dirigiste, highly disciplined, a secret cadre of ideologues dispersed throughout the nation's public and private institutions. It had relied for nearly two decades on timid obedience and the Cold War social contract. Jeyaretnam's by-election seemed to suggest something truer to authentic democracy was breaking through the palm-fringed surface of Singapore politics.

I was due to spend the Christmas of 1981 in New York. But Philip and Derek needed a cover story on the shifting political winds as soon as possible. Back to my suite at Raffles it was. From the *Review* bureau, on the thirty-ninth floor of a tower at Anson's edge, I looked across the helter-skelter of Jeyaretnam's constituency, a cubist arrangement of terra-cotta rooftops. Once again, I had a lot to learn in little time.

During the weeks I gave the reporting and writing I felt my way into a world outsiders were not meant to see. I was after the unexplored history that led to the Anson result. I needed the sociology of the discontent one rarely glimpsed behind all the tropical flora and the steel-and-glass façades in the financial district. Joshua Jeyaretnam— humane, loyal to a homespun idea of justice and a liberal stripe of social democracy—gave me all the time I wanted. Jeya was of Sri Lankan extraction and had married an Englishwoman. A widower now, he kept a portrait of her in his chambers, always with a fresh rose before it. I couldn't see his lone voice mattering as he sat opposite the ruling party's seventy-four MPs and, looked at one way, it didn't. The PAP would maul him in the years to come. But he nonetheless left a mark on the sanitized Singapore story. The American press took little interest in Jeya. Had he been a dissident in Eastern Europe, it would have lionized him.

The cover story I filed carried the headline "Politics Revived." I had found my way into the attic and basement of Washington's most presentable Asian client, there to rummage through the hidden history and the plumbing and wiring that made it work. I knew the pieces I filed just before leaving for New York, a main story and sidebars, were likely to earn ire in the Prime Minister's Office—we all did. But I had no intention of blurring reality or leaving things unsaid. It was a matter of seeing and saying to the strictest standards I had without reference to what consequences there would be.

A tumultuous year followed as Lee Kuan Yew tightened his grip. The local press was reorganized to put the government in control behind a façade of independence. It did the same with Singapore's influential labor unions. Schools began requiring instruction in "Confucian values"—filial piety, obedience, "let the lord be lordly," and so on. In Leninist fashion, the PAP redefined itself as a national movement, so declaring itself the ideological expression of the state. All the while it heckled, ridiculed, entrapped, and at one point sued Jeyaretnam, whose calm and decency were as pearls before swine next to the ruling party's abuses of the man and the law. I filed on all of it, thinking of Admiral Farragut in Mobile Bay, damning the torpedoes.

Most of us know Kundera's line in *The Book of Laughter and Forgetting*, published a few years before this time: "The struggle of man against power is the struggle of memory against forgetting." This was the lesson the year I describe, the lesson of history's intimate relation to truth. Singapore's past became a preoccupation, though it was not easy to find people willing to share memories. In time I found some who trusted me enough to talk, or who simply nursed no fear of Lee Kuan Yew's regime. I began taking a wheezing little ferry to Pulau Tekong, an outer island where dwelled Lee's longest-serving political prisoner, a fifty-year-old physician named Lim Hock Siew. Nearly two decades earlier Lim had been framed as a communist, among Lee Kuan Yew's favored political tactics, and had refused to sign one of the coerced confessions Lee required as a condition of release. Lim practiced medicine among the island's villagers and spent the rest of his time reading and missing his family. I always brought a paper bag of lychee nuts, and Lim would guide me into Singapore's political history as we threw the shells into a tiny fire he lit on damp, chill mornings. I recognized in him a very Singaporean compound of sadness and determination. "I cannot watch my children grow up," Lim said during one visit, "but neither can I give in to this man."

My favorite among the old guard was another physician. Lee Siew Choh bore a striking resemblance to Henry Miller—balding, with squinty, smiling eyes and an impish demeanor—and had a quiet practice across the street from the American Embassy. Siew Choh was encyclopedic. In the old, lost days he had been a senior figure, along with Lee Kuan Yew, in the Barisan Sosialis, the Socialist Front, which led the movement for independence. Then Kuan Yew split off, founded the People's Action Party, and began his habit of destroying anyone who might challenge the power he swiftly drew to himself. Dr. Lee, like Jeya and like Lim Hock Siew, understood what I was doing as I raked through the past. When the work exhausted me, we talked politics and history while I lay face down on his treatment table and he jabbed me with vitamin-$B^{12}$ injections. I didn't yet know it, but by this time Internal Security was following me, my telephones were tapped, and there was a government plant in the bureau. So far as I could make out, my telexes went simultaneously to Hong Kong and the Prime Minister's Office. We twice had complaints about stories we hadn't yet published.

Lee Kuan Yew had his image of a parliamentary democracy to preserve, however hollow this was widely understood to be. The rough, crude stuff one saw in Indonesia or South Korea wouldn't do. Lee's tactics by my time were not unlike those of the despot who has adversaries beaten with bags of oranges so the organs are ruined but the injuries don't show. In the custody of Internal Security goons, you stood before an air conditioner while they doused you with ice water all night. You spent your life on an outer island while your children grew up without you. My expulsion order was a matter of time, I surmised without much difficulty. When it came it was gentler but as cunning: My press visa was canceled. By then I knew the adage some departed correspondent left behind and thereafter got passed on like an amulet. "There's only one thing worse than getting it wrong in Singapore: Getting it right."

The American Embassy took an interesting role in all this. The deputy chief of mission, a genial, careful man named Mort Smith, possibly with a brief on the intelligence side, urged me to ease off after a set of tennis at his resplendent bungalow. The ambassador, Harry Thayer, was an accomplished Sinologist and a thoughtful man from a long line of diplomats. But he understood the Cold War's political exigencies. Thayer never saw me; his embassy never inquired after the American who had landed in trouble. Between a correspondent working according to accepted Western standards and a despot of proven Cold War loyalty, the choice was so obvious I could hardly call it one.

IF SINGAPORE'S WELL-TENDED GREENERY obscured a tragedy, I had seen a variant in Malaysia and in years to come would see others across the region. East Asians had lost something, just as East Europeans had, at some point before I arrived among them. Something had eluded them at the time of independence, as I was later to surmise. This was what I had first sensed while reporting in Kuala Lumpur. National aspirations had gone unmet. Diligent work was in part a question of disinterring this, the officially buried—a project made of a thousand encounters. The approved histories and the press—local or Western—told me little: They were among the essential instruments of forgetting. But I found the loss, the longing, and the true stories along the streets I walked, in the voices and demeanor of those I met, and most of all in memories, which official forgetting renders poignant but also durable.

I had cultivated an interest in the independence era since my days taking dictation from Wilfred Burchett and my graduate work at Columbia. The charismatic leaders of those postwar decades—Nehru, Nasser, Nyerere, N'krumah (my four "Ns"), along with Zhou Enlai, Sukarno, Mossadegh, Árbenz, Lumumba, others—were larger than life, the flaws of some or most notwithstanding. They expressed ideals and ambitions only those nostalgic for empire could fail to admire. We know nothing of their kind now, Mandela and Václav Havel among the few exceptions. Emerging from centuries of colonial rule and the most catastrophic war in history, they stood for an inspired vision of a commonly desired world to be achieved by way of mutual respect among nations and one or another kind of social democracy. I do not see that one can read this period otherwise. Those of a certain age I had met in Singapore—Lim Hock Siew, Lee Siew Choh, Jeyaretnam, numerous others—arose from this era and had shared its vision. Theirs, too, was that "beautifully moral and rational world" Arthur Miller came to mourn. That was who they were. The nations I was to cover during my twenty-nine years in Asia—all of them—had desired to be only what they had set out to be, neither more nor less than simply themselves. But as America pressed on toward global primacy, this admirable passion was all but extinguished. This was the tragedy I found in the eyes of so many of the Asians I was to meet and in the words of those who spoke of it. This was the object of their loss and longing.

It was difficult to report and write of these matters. Correspondents are trained to cover events, not social psychologies, a nation's under-currents, the *longue durée* of history. Foreign editors took no interest in such topics. "What happened?" was their daily preoccupation. This is the nature of "news-papers," after all. But how much better Western press coverage of Asia, and the non-West altogether, would have been had correspondents made more use of history and understood the political economy implicit in all they wrote.

America carried the Cold War to the other end of the Pacific and the rest of the developing world bearing the banner of progress. How should "primitive" people advance to the condition of modernity? The West's answer to this was as simplistic as the question itself:

"Backward" people became "modern" people by following the example of Europeans and Americans, who had invented the very idea of progress. To modernize, then, meant to Westernize. It was a matter of recreating the world in the West's image. I have long counted this among the most consequential errors of our time. We still live with it.

By the mid- to late nineteenth century, as the age of materialism displaced the Age of Reason, the West stood less for Enlightenment ideals than for the accumulation of wealth by way of science and industry. These, the modern era's measures of progress, acquired a new utility during the Cold War. If modernizing meant Westernizing, Westernizing meant accepting the free-market economic model America insisted on propagating. In the academy this was dressed up as "modernization theory." A more cravenly sycophantic bow to Cold War ideology I cannot think of, but this was how American scholars explained to Americans what their country was doing as it projected power across the Pacific. It was also the frame within which Western correspondents reported East Asia and the rest of the non-West, though few of us were sufficiently literate to understand this.

Force, violence, rampant corruption, fixed elections, and covert operations did not figure in modernization theory. In practice they proved essential to the undertaking. Authoritarian leaders were the Cold War imperative. There would have to be constitutions, parliaments, and above all elections to legitimate autocrats and dictators, who were invariably cast as "modernizers." So did Lee Kuan Yew enjoy especially vigorous American approval: He kept the window dressing tidy and the mess to a minimum.

Things were not so neat elsewhere. The Philippines was a running sore because Filipinos are a politically spirited people and the Marcos dictatorship abrogated the Cold War social contract. Sukarno wanted nothing to do with modernization theory in whatever guise it arrived. "The Bung," as he was affectionately known, was a nationalist, a "politics in command" man who understood that dignity and self-determination counted more than refrigerators and television sets. His passions were Indonesian identity and pride, democratic government however difficult and disorderly this would prove, and neutrality in the East-West conflict. "Go to hell with your foreign aid," Sukarno famously told the United States in a 1964 speech, having had enough of the political and economic strings Washington attached to its assistance programs. That was the Bung, Brother Karno. When Suharto deposed him in 1965, in a protracted coup the CIA backed, a million Indonesians (the latest figure) were murdered. Suharto's thirty-two-year presidency was ever after stained, but his New Order ("dynamic stability" was the euphemism) was modernization theory made flesh. The former general was counted a "staunch American ally," in the phrasing so often found in Western press accounts. This mattered. Ordinary Indonesians didn't. They remained an illegible blur in the American press, a great mass of indistinct Others.

By the time I arrived in Asia in 1981, Asians rarely spoke of fundamental questions such as those I have suggested, and correspondents didn't write of them. To one degree or another, public man and public space had been obliterated; the language of authentic political discourse became a kind of Latin. "Asians like money and care little for anything else" was the myth Western correspondents reproduced in their files. An Indonesian friend, full of the wistful longing I saw all around me, captured the prevailing sentiment memorably in a conversation after Suharto fell in 1998: "At first we soared like eagles, and we ended up scratching the earth like chickens."

*Mikul dhuwur mendhem jero* was among Suharto's favorite Javanese adages: "Lift high appearances, bury problems deep." Suharto understood. Like Lee Kuan Yew and others, he depended on an old habit among Americans, one served well by the cult of superficiality I first encountered at *The Times*. This was the habit of not looking too closely at the domestic doings of dictatorial allies. Most Americans did not want to see their own complicity in the violence, the deprivations, and the pernicious psychology that "modernizing" visited upon East Asians. One looked on with sorrow as America, by way of its client regimes, coerced all but the most principled among them to accept their Otherness, their inferiority—to assume that all that made them who they were was as nothing next to a bottle of Coca-Cola and a Walt Disney movie.

The press, with admirable if few exceptions, has by tradition been complicit in this collective shielding of the eyes. Some correspondents, surely, gave thought to the responsibilities they bore toward those they covered, but I cannot say overmany. They wrote and reported according to the requisite Self and Other distinctions that separated the West and the rest. There was no need to consider the people they covered in any specificity because the details of their lives were of little interest to the foreign editors to whom they filed. Hannah Arendt's pithy terminology will do nicely here: Western correspondents covering the non-West during the Cold War defactualized the story. At bottom this reflected correspondents' failure to take responsibility for themselves and their work, whether or not they reflected on these matters. They instead performed as publishers and editors required. I do not wish to be excessively critical of colleagues, and over the years I was not without sin, but these lapses—professional, intellectual, moral—were and remain difficult to excuse when we consider their consequences.

THINGS DID NOT GO WELL on my return to Hong Kong after "the island republic" expelled me. Derek stood by me when correspondents and local reporters called for comment. But you must wait until the Klieg lights are off to understand what editors are inclined to do to those who work too far beyond the fence posts. I landed ungently on the political desk as an assistant editor—a punitive assignment I was meant to understand as one. My deskbound frustrations soon got the better of me, and in a short while I made up my mind to resign.

In the *Review*'s newsroom there was little to none of the alienation journalists must accept in the American press's mainstream. My coverage on the published page was never other than what I meant to say. I had had the privilege of reporting Asia not as an Other but as itself. It is remarkable how few correspondents carry the lens of history with them. I learned at the *Review* never to travel without mine. These were gifts of value. My search through the past had been abruptly disrupted—this the very point of my expulsion. I nevertheless count leaving the *Review* among the regrettable errors of my years as a correspondent. It was unique, or nearly, in all the ways I have noted. I wish I had appreciated this earlier than I did.

I immediately put a foot wrong, naturally. When I joined *Newsweek* as a regional correspondent it was the beginning of a bad if mercifully brief dream. The magazine was the perverse exemplar of all that had gone wrong in the American press's way of covering the world. *Newsweek* was all gloss and cartoonish simplification, superficiality elevated to a commandment not much short of biblical.

Everything it published had to reflect back places and people as Cold War Americans wanted them to be. This was Arendt's defactualization as weekly editorial routine. Reporting that didn't fit the neat, usually ill-informed preconceptions of editors at Madison Avenue and East Forty-Ninth Street was killed, cut, or cavalierly mangled to fit "the story line." I used to cringe when editions arrived at each week's end. What have they done this time? No wonder the CIA found *Newsweek* an easy mark when it got the mighty Wurlitzer going.

To survive these weekly indignities I took up my old moon-lighting habit. I no longer recall how I made the connection, but I began filing to *Il Manifesto*, the Rome daily, which was (and remains) roughly equivalent to the *Guardian* during its Belfrage and Aronson years. My byline this time was Lorenzo Amato, "Lawrence the loved one," roughly—a name with an old family story behind it. It was a delight working with *Manifesto*'s editors: I dictated by telephone into a recording device and they translated and published the file in Italian. More than once this involved restoring my defiled *Newsweek* pieces to their original integrity—South Korean political repression as it was, Southeast Asia's autocrats as they were, the imposition of neoliberal economics as it was. I found poetic justice in this process. If *Newsweek* nearly killed me, to borrow Greeley's old *mot*, *Il Manifesto* helped keep me alive.

My discontent was impossible to miss, and my files didn't suit the comic-book narratives *Newsweek* wanted. When the vulgarly dapper Maynard Parker, the executive editor, came out from New York to fire me little more than a year into my service, he did so while getting measured for shirts—contrasting collars, of course—in his suite at the Mandarin. There is one satisfying detail to note about this occasion: The day before Maynard dismissed me, I and a colleague, Tracy Dahlby, had filed a long takeout on Korea that miraculously survived the abattoir in New York. It won an Overseas Press Club award for best foreign reporting a few months after my morning in Maynard's suite.

I immediately found new work with *The Christian Science Monitor*, for which I covered Hong Kong and most of Northeast Asia. And a better-run foreign desk I have never known. My editors were interested in the world as it was and as I reported it, not as they wished it or imagined it to be. This was like a spring breeze to me after the air I breathed at *Newsweek*, but *The Monitor* didn't have the budget to bring me fully on staff. I was to struggle for some time. Weeklies and monthlies whose names I no longer recall, a Canadian banking maga- zine, annual reports, advertising supplements: No freelance work was too lowly. Things took another turn in the spring of 1986, when the *International Herald Tribune* invited me into its pages. And in a short while the executive editor flew me to Paris to formalize my place at the paper.

I still remember sitting in Phil Foisie's office in the *Herald Tribune* building along the Avenue Charles-de-Gaulle in Neuilly, where the *Trib* was at the time. Phil was fond of long lunches that ended with Irish coffees (plural), and we had just finished one. I fidgeted as we went through our preliminaries. How was I going to account for the *Newsweek* debacle? I feared it would scotch my prospects.

Phil, a pleasantly rumpled man with a jowly face and a wounded sadness somewhere in his eyes, finally addressed the matter. "Well," he said, "I suppose we'd better talk about the *Newsweek* business."

"Yes," I spluttered. "I'd like to explain what…"

Phil cut me off and leaned across his desk.

"Before you go any further, I should mention how I look at this." A pause, then: "As I see it, the only good *Newsweek* correspondent is an ex-*Newsweek* correspondent."

So began a professional tie that lasted, in various capacities, twenty-one years.

I boarded my flight home as the *Trib*'s correspondent in Hong Kong, then bracing for the "handover" in 1997, when the colony was to revert to Chinese sovereignty. In time the brief expanded. I returned to Southeast Asia while also taking on the Northeast. At this point it was plain I would not rotate out of the region in the customary fashion. My new assignments meant I was to keep on in Asia and keep on learning it. This came to be a distinct advantage.

East Asia was still deep in the Cold War freeze. Suharto's Indonesia was choking on its own corruption. In the Philippines, Corazon Aquino had inspired the "People Power" revolution that toppled Ferdinand Marcos, but she was proving a "milk and cookies" president, as I wrote from Manila. In Taiwan, Chiang Ching-kuo was running the police state he had inherited it from Chiang Kai-shek, the famous generalissimo and long-serving leader of the Kuomintang. It was the same scene in South Korea. Chun Doo-hwan, the latest in the South's line of military dictators, had Kim Dae-jung and Kim Young-sam under house arrest while he suppressed the democracy movement they led. I used to visit "the two Kims" in their austerely furnished houses somewhere in Seoul's cacophonous sprawl. We spoke of their political principles and their plans for a new South Korea. K.D.J. was a figure of worldwide prominence by this time. These occasions were otherwise little different from my ferry trips in Singapore to see Lim Hock Siew on his outer island. They were variants of the same story, the Cold War story.

But the edifice Washington had built at the western end of the Pacific was crumbling, just as the Berlin Wall soon would. Marcos, Imelda, and all her shoes were forced into exile shortly after I joined the *Herald Trib*. Reading the cracks in the tortoise shell, Chun Doo-hwan ceded power in South Korea to another general two years later. Roh Tae-woo took office amid a din of demonstrations and turned out to be the liberalizing agent who saw the Korean republic out of nearly three decades of military dictatorship. Kim Young-sam and then Dae-jung succeeded him as presidents.

The most surprising turn occurred in Taiwan. Under Chiang Ching-kuo, the Republic of China was an anachronism in black and white, a leftover from the late nineteen forties. The Kuomintang's infamous connections to Chinese crime syndicates still lay in the background, as did the secret police. Then came a stunner out of nowhere. Late in 1985, Chiang *fils* had declared in a Constitution Day speech that he would be the last Chiang to hold the presidency: The next president would be chosen in free elections. Two years later he ended thirty-eight years of martial law, dating to the Kuomintang's retreat from the mainland a few months before Mao took Beijing in October 1949.

The aging Chiang died a year later. At the end of his life he had set in motion a democratization process that had never featured in the Chiang family's political repertoire. In a short time, freshly and fairly elected lawmakers were breaking out in brawls on the floor of the Legislative Yuan. I soon enough saw the same in Seoul. I read these extraordinary events as a salutary celebration of release from prisons whose guards were local hires but whose superintendents resided in Washington.

The *Trib*, like the *Review*, was an oddity. It was American-owned but did not have altogether the soul of an American newspaper. The newsroom was in Paris and the readership worldwide. The *Trib* had few correspondents of its own—I was one of a half-dozen or so—and we enjoyed a subtle immunity from the usual ideological imperatives. This was not so for others appearing in the paper. At this time, *The New York Times* and *The Washington Post* had equal shares of *Trib* stock, and much of the news hole was filled with pieces picked up from these two dailies. It made for awkward juxtapositions. I was writing for Asians and Europeans as much as anyone else and took no interest in Cold War ideology; the *Post* and *Times* copy that arrived in Paris overnight was written for Americans and was bound by the familiar rigidities. In later years this peculiarity would lead to frictions with "the cousins" in the *Times* and *Post* bureaus.

By 1987, the late John Vinocur, a former *Times* correspondent and an accomplished Europeanist, had replaced Phil Foisie as executive editor. That summer John called me to Paris to attend celebrations of the *Trib*'s centenary. There was a sprawling dinner party at the Trocadéro, the Eiffel Tower opposite lit in the paper's honor. All Paris was there. (Leslie Caron, as lovely at fifty-odd as she was in *Fanny* and *The L-Shaped Room*, graced our table.) The following evening, John approached me at Le Village, the bistro downstairs from the newsroom. "I'm opening a bureau in Tokyo," he said in the blunt manner he favored. "Will you go?" My plane put down at Narita a few months later.

Shortly after the 1945 surrender, Washington set about fashioning Japan as its first and most important East Asian satellite, the model for all the others. Cold Warriors pushed aside the principled New Dealers who had planned the Occupation, setting in motion what is called "the reverse course." War criminals were reinvented as well-meaning modernizers. Elections were fixed with CIA assistance and organized labor crushed. Washington funneled extravagant sums to the corrupt but pliant Liberal Democratic Party, a covert operation that endured for decades. The group of scholars who prettified this disgrace for Americans—Edwin Reischauer their high priest, Ezra Vogel a prominent prelate—were known contemptuously among the better Japanists as the Chrysanthemum Club after the imperial seal; its members were called *geisha*. For correspondents in Tokyo the *geisha*'s books were bedrock reading, and it showed in the American press's nonstop drivel depicting a placid-as-a-pond nation of industrious workers happily dedicated to "the Japanese miracle." I went through the same books prior to my arrival. The first thing I noted as I settled in Tokyo was that the people and the nation I'd read about had nothing to do with the people and the nation I saw from my bureau's windows. The Japanese draw a distinction between the *omote* and *ura* of things—the presented imagery and the inner reality. The books I had read and the coverage I had started to follow were all about the *omote* of modern Japan, leaving its *ura*, its hidden truths, by and large untouched.

For a long time, one was sent to Tokyo to cover the land of the nothing new. Little ever changed. Then suddenly more or less everything did. Japan fulfilled its longtime dream, "catching up to the West," just as I arrived. It would have to find some other purpose to drive it forward. Then the Cold War at last drew to a close, shredding all the assumptions of the previous four decades. Between these two momentous events came a third: Hirohito died. For many years his lingering presence—the Americans had reinvented him, too—had kept the Japanese locked in the past, unable to see it clearly, unable to put history in its proper place. Instantly after the emperor's death in January 1989, shedding the past's burdens and discovering how to live creatively in the present was precisely the national project.

I had opened the bureau in the *Mainichi Shimbun* building opposite the Imperial Palace. It was another bit of good fortune that I was able to watch Japan from this perch during these exceptional years. I was present as the first stone America laid in its Cold War edifice across the Pacific broke into pieces. With palpable unease, the nation that had taken Washington's orders the whole of the postwar era was unsteadily feeling its way—learning, if cautiously, to think for itself. Japan was radically underdeveloped in its political life, as all the satellites were. It went through six premiers during my tour and would get through five more before century's end. After decades of Liberal Democratic rule, a Socialist took office in 1994. He was followed by Ryūtarō Hashimoto, who I admired and with whom I got along well. Scion of an old political family, Hashimoto was a Gaullist in Tokyo's borrowed political parlance, favoring cordial but more distant relations with the United States. It is an aspiration yet to be realized, to my disappointment.

While I was running the *Trib*'s bureau, I also began writing "Letter from Tokyo" for *The New Yorker*. This was with the encouragement of the late Bob Shaplen, the magazine's longtime correspondent in Asia. I had met Shaplen during a weekend back in Hong Kong, and he kindly pushed me in the direction of Bob Gottlieb, who had succeeded the celebrated William Shawn in the editor's chair. Gottlieb and I got on well, and I welcomed the chance to file from Japan at length and with the kind of nuance it is impossible to get into a daily newspaper. Japan in the late eighties and early nineties warranted this kind of work: It was time Americans understood Japan and its people as more than a nation of transistor salesmen, as de Gaulle had indelicately put it in 1962. My "Letters," alas, lasted as long as Gottlieb's tenure, a matter of a few years, but those pieces taught me the imperative of understanding how the world looked from the perspectives of others.

Here I must relate events that would surely warrant an entry in the annals of foreign correspondence were there any such thing. They are a measure of the hold American orthodoxy had over the correspondents the big dailies sent abroad, and the shrinking space available to those who worked independently of it.

Some years into my tour in Tokyo, an order came from Paris: Turn your attention to different sorts of stories—stock-market stories, corporate stories, culture stories if you're so inclined. An apparently bottomless corruption scandal was then shaking Nagata-chō, Tokyo's political quarter, to its foundations. The decades-old system of "money politics," just as America had cultivated it, was at last coming unstuck. "No need to bother with that stuff," I was advised.

Nonplussed is too mild a term for my reaction. "Unprecedented" is—or was then—a word you avoided as a matter of craft: For the careful correspondent it can prove a treacherous adjective. But if I were ordered to stop filing important stories, this was surely a one-of-a-kind moment in my professional life.

I back-channeled with a trusted editor in Paris.

"What's this, Sam?" Sam Abt was the longtime news editor and a friend. "I've got these stories bolted down. You're fronting me every day."

"You've got them in hand and we're fronting you. Now go quiet and think about other things." Sam knew trouble when he saw it, wanted me to survive at the paper, and this was the best advice he could give me.

It soon transpired by way of another editor that my cousins at *The Times* had begun to grouse to the foreign desk on West Forty-Third Street that I was too often on page one of my newspaper and they not on it often enough. There was a good reason for this, and I've already suggested it. The *Trib* arrived on Tokyo doorsteps and at newsagents six days a week. I was writing for these readers as much as I was for someone in Brussels or Madrid. *The Times*'s coverage told readers in Japan little that they didn't already know, often a few days previously. It was off-kilter, out of step. Nonetheless, *The Times*'s Tokyo bureau chief was complaining to the foreign editor in New York, who was in turn leaning on Paris. Setting aside the tiresome vanity one must tolerate in most *Times* correspondents, this was at bottom a conflict of perspectives—the cousins insisting that in the breach America's had to prevail.

A few days after my stinging directive from Paris, my editors managed to push me straight into a hall of mirrors. There had been an important break in the corruption scandal, which was worldwide news at that point, and it had come late in the day Tokyo time. The *Times* and *Post* bureaus were indisposed. Could I file? Six hundred words would do.

It was a bitter moment. "Take wires," I told Sam when he called. "I've stopped paying attention by order of my editors."

My years as a *Trib* correspondent across the region proved my last as an independent correspondent working in the mainstream. There would be many more as a contributor to the opinion page; I was later brought back to edit the news pages of the Asian edition. But I had had a brief taste of post–Cold War American journalism and found it vinegar. I chose the moment to hang up the trench coat—though not for the last time, alas.

AMERICA'S EXPORT of neoliberal ideology into a world with very different aspirations amounted to a revolution as ambitious as that commonly assigned to the Communist International. The political economy imposed on others during the Cold War decades was an instrument of power deployed without reference to cultures, histories, traditions, or anything else authentically native to any given nation. This amounted to the Self and Other discourse taken to its extreme, the *mission civilisatrice* made new. One recognized all the old presumptions—material superiority, racial superiority, cultural superiority, an exceptional nation's superior way at all things. Correspondents were as given to this consciousness as anyone else and were no better able to stand outside it. In this way the Cold War did more damage to foreign news coverage than any other event in the second half of the twentieth century.

My decades as a correspondent left me with essential questions: Must a correspondent's work remain always embedded in his or her culture or nationality? Must it reflect the assumptions and presuppositions, the politics and political positioning, of the medium for which he reports? Or can the work transform the correspondent such that he is more than an American writing for an American newspaper, or an Egyptian writing for an Egyptian newspaper, or (not infrequently the case now) an Egyptian or Brazilian reporting for American, British, or who-have-you media? These are not musings: They arose directly from my years at the *Far Eastern Economic Review*, my brief but rewarding time with *The Christian Science Monitor*, and the *International Herald Tribune*. I count them vital questions now.

The readily available reply to this last thought is negative. Taking the past as a guide, it is a shared point of view that defines a culture, and this cannot be surrendered. If you report for an American newspaper you are tattooed "American" and your work, by the time it is published, speaks in the tongue, the unspoken language hidden within all languages. But my years in the field suggested another answer. Of all that our time has to tell us, first among its messages is that the past is only so useful as a tool of navigation. High among our tasks is a purposeful, continual act of transcendence—of ourselves, of our inherited perspectives, of our cultures. In hindsight this is what I admired most in Wilfred Burchett. There was no Self and Other in Wilfred's work. It is what I admired in John Hersey's *Hiroshima* and in Herbert Matthews's celebrated reports from Cuba for *The New York Times*. But these correspondents were among the exceptions proving their century's rule. Self and Other still defined the correspondent's work in their time. The task facing publishers, editors, and correspondents now at work is to make the exceptional in the twentieth century the norm in the twenty-first. We are not there yet, to put the point mildly.

In later years, while lecturing at The University of Hong Kong, I wrote a course called "Reinventing 'the Foreign Correspondent.'" It derived from my years in the field and the questions with which those years left me. This is our project now. Who correspondents are, what they do and how, where they stand in relation to those they are covering, their responsibility to those they cover as well to their readers or viewers—all this requires a fundamental rethink, if these questions have until now been thought of at all. Going native, once a transgression, is to be counted not merely a virtue but an imperative. It means drawing much closer than tradition has allowed to erase the imaginary borderline between Self and Other. It means understanding the cult of superficiality as an ideological construct. It means leaving part of oneself behind for the sake of the assignment. It means reporting another people not with one's nose pressed against glass but, after determined effort, from within, from among them. Nietzsche called this taking off the garb of the West. Havel, in a noted speech delivered at Independence Hall in Philadelphia on 4 July 1994, called what I describe "a new model of coëxistence, based on man's transcending himself." After a long time at this correspondents will realize, as I did, that in covering others they are staring into a mirror—there to learn as much about themselves as those to whom they pose incessant questions.

I describe a generation's project and harbor no illusions as to how difficult it will be to accomplish this transformation. I take this difficulty as the measure of things: However formidable the summons or great the resistance to be encountered, it is precisely to this extent correspondents and editors must set about getting it done. This, too, is a responsibility. In modest respects, the best now in the field, a special few, have begun to assume it. Two decades into our new century, are they to remain indefinitely the craft's exceptions?

# 3.

# 'Nobody Believes Anything.'

> The reporter's task is to find a way
> of weaving these threads of unreality
> into a fabric that the reader will not
> recognize as entirely unreal.
>
> ———Daniel Boorstin,
> *The Image,*
> 1962.

ALL OF US ABLE TO RECALL the events of 11 September 2001 know where we were, surely, as the hours unfolded that fateful day. In this, the attacks in New York and Washington resembled the Kennedy assassination thirty-eight autumns earlier. Each occasion marked a sudden loss. Each imposed a difficult self-examination upon us. Who were we that such tragedies had befallen us? Were we other than who and what we thought we were?

I lived in a decrepit but beloved farmhouse in northwest Connecticut at the turn of our century. That morning I was writing a column for Bloomberg News, where I was then under contract. I scrubbed the piece and did my best to address the events to hand. "Some historic turn has occurred this week in America's relations with the rest of the world. Of this we can be certain," I began. "But of what nature? No certainty there. And of what consequence? None there either." This same surmise of an abrupt bend in our thinking and our trajectory applied, I soon saw, to our relations with ourselves and to what we told ourselves about ourselves, not least by way of our press.

There would be a turn in journalism, too, and from where we sit now we can count it similarly historic.

All day the radio broadcast the disbelieving voices of reporters describing the scenes in lower Manhattan and at the Pentagon. For many days, television news looped the footage of those moments when planes struck the World Trade Center towers and the smoke began to billow. The wreckage we obsessively showed ourselves was an objective correlative, it seemed to me. The blows of greatest magnitude were to our minds and hearts.

"One thought of history as something rather unpleasant that happened to other people," Toynbee wrote in a recollection of his childhood in late-imperial Britain. It is not a rational presumption, but its power cannot be overstated. When the first English settlers crossed the Atlantic in the early seventeenth century, they, too, understood themselves to have escaped history—the Old World's sordid, decadent story. The thought has endured in the American consciousness: To be immune from history and the ravages of time is the essence of our claim to exceptionalism. This has long been reflected in the way our media reports on the rest of the world, a world ever vulnerable to corruption and decline as America is not. Hence the ineffable injury of that instant when Americans found themselves thrust into time and history, no longer outside of either. They were "dis-illusioned." This was the shock that day delivered, the shock that lingers still.

I hold to 11 September as the day the American century ended. Tragic as were the fatalities, the greater deaths were of spirit, of belief in ourselves and our story. And to cite Toynbee again, it is spiritual collapses, as against external events, that send civilizations into decline. Americans manifested a hyperventilated patriotism as the news on 11 September flickered across their television screens. But it was hard to miss the want of confidence in this nationalistic swell. There was something of performance, of spectacle, in all those tiny flags on sticks and in shop windows. They seemed to me a way people had of holding onto a past that had just passed. The fundamental collapse on 11 September was of that faith that had driven Americans for nearly four centuries, not least faith in our righteousness before all others. We have ever since merely pretended to this faith and the certainty it once conferred. Desperation has defined us.

I refer again to Arthur Miller's remarkable "The Year It Came Apart," his thoughts on 1949 from the perspective of the mid-nineteen seventies. "An inner sense of direction, a moral compass, shuttered," he wrote. We can read this now as an early intimation of our time. Gradually at first and then not so, ordinary notions of proper conduct, of ethics to be observed, of standards of all sorts, have lapsed. This is certainly evident in America's conduct abroad since 2001, ever more of which is obscured from public view. It is as certainly so of the practice of journalism, our press having been instrumental in the obscuring. In the years since 2001 American media have descended into a condition worse, in my estimation, than the worst of the Cold War decades. The horizontal coordination and control of information and "messaging" across the government, the corporations, and the media is now—the word seems apt this time—unprecedented. A regime of censorship falls upon society like dusk in late autumn. I trace this abandonment of principle to that otherwise fine morning now two decades and two years behind us. The crisis in our media that is evident now cannot be understood separately from the crisis into which the national security state has fallen. This could not be otherwise, given the long and inti-mate relationship between the two.

Some Americans ruminated for a brief and special time after 11 September. The best among us at last looked honestly at the milieu out of which the attacks had arisen. Poverty, disease and malnutrition, poor schools or none, despotic rulers, pervasive corruption, hopeless-ness, desperation: What had America done, notably but not only in the Middle East, to create and sustain these conditions and what should America do now to address them? I have ever since counted those months a credit to Americans. They seemed—for a short while—pref-ace to a fundamental change in our self-awareness and direction. We would see differently. Our media would report the world differently such that we could finally open our eyes to it. Context, causality, human agency, historic responsibility: They would give readers these things as previously they had not. I saw suggestions of this in the post–11 September coverage—not overmany, but some. Then came George W. Bush's first State of the Union address, delivered on 29 January 2002. A year and ten days into his presidency, Bush drew a line under all such thinking as he declared his "axis of evil"—at that time consisting of Iraq, Iran, and North Korea—against which we were at war. The media's conformity to this new turn is high among their post–11 September errors—and the source of various others.

My first column after Bush's speech carried the headline, "An Axis of Idiocy: The State of Bush's World." It was a lament written from the middle of me in little more than an hour. "I lived through the 1950s once, and once was once more than enough," it began. "After 11 long years in the desert, a decade and some without serious enemies, the good times are back, and the Bush administration is dedicated above all to prolonging them." Bloomberg published the piece the evening of 2 February. My telephone rang at one o'clock the following morning. It was Matt Winkler, at the time Bloomberg's notoriously unpleasant editor in chief, threatening to fire me. A year later he did. I should have considered then whether a new generation of Arthur Hays Sulzbergers and Bill Paleys was upon us.

Maybe all nations, as they choose unconsciously what to remember and what to forget or blot out, agree within themselves as to what can be said and what cannot. Ernest Renan and others, notably the French, have in the past argued persuasively that these silent agreements as to the parameters of memory are part of what binds a people together. "Forgetting, I would say even historical error, is an essential factor in the creation of a nation," Renan wrote in *Qu'est-ce qu'une nation?* ("What Is a Nation?"), an 1882 lecture he delivered at the Sorbonne. One cannot approve of this thought as it applies to any people, true as it may be. But Americans draw this line between the sayable and unsayable more severely than anyone else, it has long seemed to me. De Tocqueville was pithy on this point: "I know of no country," he wrote in the first volume of *Democracy in America*, "in which there is so little independence of mind and real freedom of discussion as in America."

That after-midnight telephone call in response to a toughly worded but perfectly defensible commentary was a first taste of how the press was to conduct itself in the post-2001 era. America has had no need of censors in the way we think of them in authoritarian contexts—at least until now, I have to add. The censored have by a long tradition done all the self-censoring required to control the narrative, to counter our "dis-illusioning," to reassure us we are still and always safe from history's tempests. Among corporate-owned media this remains the case; it is digital media platforms and those who use them to write independently of power that have pushed America into its current phase—and may it prove a phase—of overt censorship.

Nobody working in mainstream media today speaks of a loss of belief in the purpose a vigorous press is assigned in a democratic society. But a press that is effectively government-supervised is a press in name only. The profession's forms remain, but it has abandoned its responsibilities. The craft is a shadow cast by what it once purported to be. The only exceptions in this are among what we call "alternative media"—a term to which I have objected since those days I used to pause to look up at the Noguchi bas-relief at The Associated Press Building in Manhattan.

To me, the question as I write these chapters is whether and how American newspapers and broadcasters will recover from the delinquencies that began in the days after 11 September. Such a recovery is not out of the question, but let us not misplace our hopes: My intent is to give a history to the crisis confronting journalists, and history holds little promise. Our time is the time of the few who turn on those with whom they once stood. Our time belongs to the wanderers among us.

THE DEBRIS IN LOWER MANHATTAN was still settling when Ari Fleischer, President Bush's press secretary, arranged a conference call with America's leading editors in Washington, those who controlled what did and did not go into the press's daily report from the capital. Fleischer's intent was to secure the cooperation of newspapers and broadcasters as the administration defined and prosecuted its new "war on terror." He asked those on the line to black out coverage that revealed how America would wage this war. Fleischer was specifically eager to keep from public view the operations of the CIA and the rest of the national security apparatus. All present that day readily obliged the Bush administration in these matters.

When a White House press secretary considers it proper to convene such a gathering and ask those present to participate in the censorship of their own publications, it is plain that the press's relationship to power—in this case political and administrative power—was already compromised. We cannot but wonder that the editors to whom Fleischer appealed soon after accepted the term "war on terror" with no recorded hesitation or objection. I count this in-unison response a defining moment of the post-2001 years. Just as they did during the Cold War, American media once again redefined their role. Let us not underestimate the significance here. To adopt the language of war would soon implicate the press in all manner of legal and ethical breaches—the invasion of Iraq, CIA torture sites and the abuses at Guantánamo, drone assassinations, various "regime changes," the new term for coups so as to protect American readers and viewers from the reality of what their nation was doing.

Jill Abramson, *The New York Times*'s Washington bureau chief at the time, has given us what seems the only extant account of the conference call with Fleischer. "The purpose of the call was to make an agreement with the press—this was just days after 9.11—that we not publish any stories that would go into details about the sources and methods of our intelligence programs," Abramson explained some years later. "It wasn't complicated to withhold such information. And for some years, really quite a few years, I don't think the press, in general, did publish any stories that upset the Bush White House or seemed to breach that agreement." Reporting on questions of war and national security would thenceforth require extravagant measures of defactualization, to make this point more plainly. The universe of the unsayable would grow ever larger.

There is a reason Abramson chose to speak so forthrightly when, in the summer of 2014, she addressed the Chautauqua Institution, an old convocation of the well-intended in upstate New York: She had just been fired as *The Times*'s executive editor. Abramson remained loyal to the paper after her dismissal, but it was as if, at Chautauqua a few months later, some nondisclosure pact had expired. "Because I am not at *The Times* anymore," she said in a curious aside, "I can really be a little bit more candid and honest with you about my thoughts about how the press has handled these stories going back over time." There is no "more honest" or "less honest" in journalism, I am compelled to point out: These notions are for attorneys and politicians. In journalism there is only honesty and dishonesty, and we find some of each in Abramson's speech. Her remarks are nonetheless worth considering in detail. In them she acknowledges, I detect unconsciously, media's complicity as the national security state sequesters itself ever more thoroughly from public scrutiny. We find an identification with power that is presumed to require no explanation or defense.

The consequences of the relationship Abramson described were calamitously evident in ensuing years. The largest and costliest of these was the 2003 invasion of Iraq, justified by infamously false intelligence reports *The Times* was instrumental in disseminating. That same year the American press neglected the tortures at Abu Ghraib prison until Seymour Hersh's investigative work made it impossible to avoid reporting them any longer. A year later *The Times* determined to withhold a report on the National Security Agency's illegal wiretapping programs. *The Times* published the piece only when James Risen, who wrote it, forced its hand a year later by including his report in a book he was about to publish.

Abramson noted another case of withheld reporting in her Chautauqua presentation. In 2013 *The Times* was about to publish a piece on intelligence intercepts between two purported leaders of al-Qaeda. Just prior to running it, Abramson, by this time executive editor, took a call from James Clapper, then director of national intelligence. "Jill Abramson, you will have blood on your hands if *The Times* publishes this story," Clapper, by Abramson's account, barked into her cellular telephone. Abramson held the story; McClatchy newspapers ran it two days later. Nobody's hands were bloodied, and we now know as a matter of record that by 2013 the Obama administration had covertly allied with al-Qaeda in their common cause to bring down the Syrian government. In Abramson's explanation of the decision she made we recognize the intellectual, professional, and moral laxity that proves a prevalent characteristic of the American press in the post–11 September period.

"When someone says, 'You'll have blood on your hands,' you pause and take it very seriously," Abramson told her Chautauqua audience. This is incontrovertibly so. And the first thing the serious professional does is ask, *Who is saying this and why?* Then one must consider that person's record in the way of lies and truths, and Clapper's is indefensible. Then: *Is it my responsibility to keep government secrets, or does my work lie in the opposite direction?* And at last: *Are my hands the hands at issue?* An ordinary City Hall reporter would pose elementary questions of this sort. Abramson considered none of them, and I doubt any other senior editor with James Clapper on the line would have done any differently. In the post–11 September era, one does not question the word of those in authority, including intelligence agencies with long records of deceit. This is why journalists covering Washington today find themselves so often reproducing mis- and disinformation. This is how they are reduced to serving as the clerks of the governing class, and their newspapers to official bulletin boards. I do not consider these characterizations overstated.

"Journalists are Americans, too," Abramson said in defense of the agreement reached with Ari Fleischer. "I consider myself, like I'm sure many of you do, to be a patriot." To be honest, I found it shocking to listen to this portion of Abramson's speech via the audio recording Chautauqua makes available on its website. It is a straight readout of explanations the Alsop brothers and numerous others marshaled to excuse their collusion with power during the Cold War decades. The same flaccid logic applies: To be a good American, one must sometimes abandon the press's fundamental principles. This had landed journalists and journalism in trouble in the nineteen fifties and sixties and would land them in as much or more this time.

The curtain of national security has been drawn ever more firmly since 2001. As a careful reader can detect in the foreign reports of the leading dailies, the press now serves as the guardian of the *arcana imperii*, the secrets empire holds close so as to proceed without objection. This practice is not without direct consequences. How many lives would have been spared, how much suffering and destruction avoided, had Abramson and her colleagues held official accounts of Iraq's weapons of mass destruction up to the light? Ditto, on a smaller scale, had they investigated, sooner than they did, the atrocities at Abu Ghraib prison as the Pentagon sought to cover them up. What constraints could the press have forced had it vigorously scrutinized the NSA's surveillance programs when early indications of them began to emerge? There are many other such cases. It is now well-established, another matter of record, that Washington spent years and hundreds of millions of dollars supporting not just al-Qaeda but numerous of the murderous jihadist militias active in Syria in the interest of its coup operation against the secular government in Damascus. Well-established, a matter of record, but still unreported in corporate media. The American press does have blood on its hands, a great deal of it one could argue, precisely because it succumbed repeatedly to the James Clappers populating Washington as they coerced editors and reporters to take their part in the war on terror and all that has arisen in consequence of it.

Before *The Times* dismissed her, Jill Abramson was a journalist of very high stature, if not of high caliber. I do not single her out to suggest she was a prime mover in the American press's post-2001 malaise or bore more responsibility than numerous others. Hers is merely an exemplary case. Her thoughts, decisions, justifications, illusions—these ran through the profession, as they continue to do. Abramson in professional exile simply spoke more openly than her colleagues, nearly all of whom remain silent on the matters she raised.

So often, I find, the most interesting things people have to tell us are the things they tell us without intending to. We understand from Abramson's Chautauqua speech that the press learned nothing from its Cold War compromises. It made precisely these mistakes again after 11 September because it never summoned the integrity to face its earlier wrongs. The subtext of Abramson's presentation was that *The Times* had self-corrected by the time she spoke, an idea of vindication shared among American media. Past evils, once again, had passed. The record attests otherwise very plainly. Apart from the specific cases I note in these pages, we have no sound reporting on Russia, its leaders, and their statements or intentions, on China and its leaders, on Iran, on the war in Ukraine that rages as I write. Were we to conduct our own "test of the news," a century after Lippmann and Merz's, the outcome would be the same: "They were derelict in that duty."

As Abramson reminds us, we have acquiesced over some decades now as our culture has transformed rational inquiry into rationalization. Thought is instrumentalized: It has no inherent value other than its service to one's purpose. Disinterest is the notion of another time, little understood in ours. Logic gives way to motivated logic. Max Horkheimer examined this, the triumph of self-interest, with acuity in *The Eclipse of Reason*, a now-overlooked essay he published in 1947, and we do well to note the year. "Reason as an organ for perceiving the true nature of reality and determining the guiding principles of our lives," Horkheimer wrote, "has come to be regarded as obsolete." This "surrender to the 'irrational'" does great damage to the surrendering society, as is evident as we look out our windows. It is near to fatal for the practice of journalism, Jill Abramson merely an illustrative case.

A remarkable example of the media's relapse into old habits came to light in 2008. In the spring of that year *The New York Times,* notwithstanding its own very numerous compromises with power, published an investigation into the television networks' post-2001 practice of hiring former military officers as on-air analysts without disclosing fully who they were or their interests in the direction of American policy. These hires came to several dozen at all the networks, CNN the worst offender among them. Their undisclosed interests often included ties to military contractors benefiting from the wars in Afghanistan and Iraq. Selling those wars to maintain public support for them was an urgent task. As one of *The Times*'s sources explained, "This was a coherent, active policy."

The broadcasters have further embraced this practice since *The Times* reported it. Television viewers are now offered former CIA directors and senior officers, top NSA officials, and other representatives of the national security state as legitimate, balanced commentators on news events. All the deceptions first evident when broadcasters were young in the late nineteen forties are evident once again. The networks make the same effort to present these people as disinterested analysts. Cultivating the appearance of objectivity and obscuring conflicts of interest are standard practices. And we find the viewing public once again averting its eyes out of the same need to believe that the media they count on to inform them are free, are independent, are principled. The only good news here is that a sharply declining percentage of the public is given to this kind of flinching.

If the American press since 11 September resembles what it made of itself during the Cold War, it is more than a mirror image. The wrongs of the past were measured against ideals and principles that were still acknowledged even if they were often abused or ignored. With some exceptions, transgressions were judged as transgressions. This is no longer so. Derelictions and compromises are in our time institutionalized by way of a redefinition of the craft that is evident if unstated. The press's proximity to power was once understood as a breach, however little was done to rectify it. Journalists now presume their legitimacy derives from their service as power's appendages: This is implicit in much of their work. They have at last accepted Kennedy's post–Bay of Pigs entreaty: Coverage of important foreign affairs questions is routinely subject to the criterion of national security.

Here I draw a critical distinction, again with a Cold War echo. In the *New York Times* report just noted, cooperation with the national security state was not at issue. In my reading, *The Times* wrote critically of the networks' use of former generals and intelligence officials because the arrangement was too visible for *The Times*'s taste. *The Times* routinely checks its copy with government officials before going to press when secrets or matters of national security are at issue. *Times* and *Washington Post* correspondents routinely accept fellowships at research institutions funded by defense contractors and appendages of the national security state, entities they are charged with reporting upon. The list of such conflicting interests, which are acknowledged only if exposed, is long. To its credit, *The Los Angeles Times* fired a reporter named Ken Dilanian in September 2014, when he was publicly identified as a CIA collaborator. Three months later, NBC News hired him to cover the intelligence agencies and national security.

I see but one way to account for the post–11 September condition of our press. The era of America's global dominion now passes. I nominate this as the greatest of our twenty-first century's unsayables. The crouch those who wield American power assumed in the autumn of 2001—defensive and aggressive all at once—remains their posture. Our press's performance cannot be understood separately from these realities. A great deal of its purpose now is to keep the unsayable unsaid.

FATE ARRIVED AT MY AGED FARM a couple of years after the events of 11 September. Bloomberg sent me a pink slip after Singapore—nemesis once again—sued for one of my commentaries on patently specious grounds. Then the domestic ménage came undone. Reluctantly and with no idea of what would come next, I made up my mind to sell Grant Farm. When I drove out of the barnyard for the last time, I reflected, I would have no more reason to turn right than I would left. I do not recommend the circumstance.

One blustery March morning shortly before my final departure, the telephone rang. It was Walter Wells, the *International Herald Tribune*'s longtime managing editor. Wells and I had known each other for many years. He was about to be named the *Trib*'s new executive editor. Would I consider coming to Paris? Pinning your hopes on a *deus ex machina* is surely the most forlorn of strategies, but a *deus* descended from the *machina* just when I needed it. I had no desire to return to daily work: I was writing essays and books by this time. But I would get nothing of worth done for a good while in my state of distracted grief. I landed at Paris–Charles de Gaulle a few weeks after closing on the farm.

For most of those months in Paris I had no idea why Walter had called me over. I was on the copy desk and didn't know quite why. Line editing was a task I could manage proficiently, having done so much of it in earlier days, but so could many others who were younger and less expensive than I. One day in the autumn, Walter took me to lunch. We bantered and reminisced. Then he told me about a new plan. The paper was launching an Asian edition, with a full-dress newsroom in Hong Kong. Would I like to edit its news pages? I wouldn't, in my heart of hearts. Climbing the management ladder had never interested me, and residing in Hong Kong again interested me even less. But my own work, as noted, was a fallow field. I arrived back in the territory during what were for me the empty days between Christmas and New Year's, 2004 turning into 2005.

This was a not-quite-legible moment at the *Herald Tribune*. A short time before Walter called me, *The Times* had bought out *The Washington Post*'s half of the *Trib* for seventy million dollars. As everyone at both papers understood, New York had confronted Washington with an elbows-out offer it couldn't refuse: Sell us your stock or we'll start an international edition of our own, and that will be the end of the *Trib*. All had held steady, but there were pennies yet to drop. So they began to do soon after I arrived in Hong Kong. In due course the long- and much-beloved *Herald Tribune* no longer seemed itself. Not even its name would survive its *Times*ification. Nor would I.

My principal tasks were two as I ran the news pages. An imposing pile of pieces from *New York Times* reporters awaited me each morning. I chose the best of them, whittled them to fit the *Trib*'s much smaller news hole, and sent them to the copy desk. *Times* copy was "pre-chewed"—it had already been edited once in New York. Selection was important, but this otherwise amounted to editing with a shovel and was, indeed, as inspiring as digging a ditch.

While Walter Wells and I were negotiating my appointment in Paris, he planned a ten-day swing through Asia looking for correspondents who would file directly to me in Hong Kong, bringing the paper closer to the ground across the region. I remember standing at the edge of the newsroom one afternoon and advising Walter to step carefully. "Beware the 'strolling players,'" I said, "the poseurs and barely competent freelancers. Let's not rush." Walter, who seemed determined to keep me at bay during this recruitment effort, rushed. He returned to Paris and handed me a crew of correspondents who were now either *Trib* staff or under contract on one or another set of terms. These were mine to manage—my second daily task.

It was a pleasure working with the best of these people. Choe Sang-hun, our Seoul correspondent, had many years at The Associated Press behind him. Sang-hun had to transition from stripped-down agency copy—marching paragraphs, I called the standard wire-service file—to the crafted, carefully interpretive writing I wanted. He did so in no time and later went on to file from Seoul for *The Times*. Carlos Condé, our man in Manila, had more to learn and learned it attentively. Anand Ghiridharadas brought a good mind and a literary command of language to his bureau in Bombay. Anand, who in my estimation was never meant for the rigors and limitations of daily work, wrote too much: He once gave me on the order of seven thousand words to meet a fifteen-hundred-word assignment. But what Anand wrote was some of the best work I got out of my correspondents.

There were others whose files consistently came up to the standard to which I held them. And then there were ... others.

Walter had landed me with a few strolling players, and these I managed as best I could. Some came along in time; others were no-hopers to whom I devoted as little effort as possible, beating their copy into minimally acceptable shape in the manner of a rewrite man in the old mold. There were two correspondents of this latter sort who warrant scrutiny here. Neither had any training as foreign correspondents so far as I could make out. Both were Australian. One had a background in military intelligence, courtesy of which he spoke middling Mandarin; the other, also an army veteran, was a mystery to me. He seemed to have dropped from the sky into the profession. Both wrote poorly and neither wrote often—one of them no more than once a month or so, an unheard-of pace for a staff correspondent.

Readers may by now guess where I am headed. My suspicion that I had two intelligence operatives on my staff took root soon after

I began working with my Australian contingent. In time this grew into a certainty. Here I note that, to an extent one would not expect, compromised correspondents often make little effort among colleagues to disguise their true identities. What these two were up to was not much short of common knowledge around the bar at the Foreign Correspondents' Club. They were of a piece with what one already knew of the Australians. Southeast Asia is their Caribbean; they are minutely concerned with China's emergence as a Pacific power. Their intelligence services are consequently thick on the ground across the region.

Why had Walter Wells hired these two, whose competence was at best minimal? Given how well I knew the scene, why had he kept me out of the vetting process? There seems only one sensible answer to this, and it is the last thing I wish to accept as so. Nobody in Paris appeared to think these hires were at all odd. I did—and then I didn't. The thought that intelligence and the press had angelically disengaged in observance of democratic proprieties after the Church Committee finished its work had never struck me as credible. Now I was in an editor's chair—not senior enough to be let in on the protocol but senior enough to suspect I witnessed it firsthand.

I pondered in silence. It is a not-done among journalists to suggest publicly that a colleague is working for an intelligence agency. Livelihoods and lives can be ruined, so it is an ethical question. You do not announce your *j'accuse* without evidence, and evidence in these sorts of cases is almost impossible to come by. Mine was the same silence correspondents and editors had observed when the profession opened itself to contamination in the nineteen fifties and sixties. I shall continue to observe it: No names.

The *Herald Tribune* had a history in this line, although we cannot count it more than a collection of highly suggestive curiosities. Phil Foisie, before he took the executive editor's chair in Paris, was celebrated for building a foreign desk at *The Washington Post*, a something-from-nothing endeavor. But there was more to Foisie than a passion for foreign news, long lunches, and Irish coffees. After finishing at Harvard, he had served as a military intelligence officer attached to Chiang Kai-shek's Nationalist Army. He stayed on in China after the war, working for a couple of relief agencies and as city editor at the *China Press*, an English-language daily in Shanghai—all good "covers," if that is what they were. Later in life, post-*Trib*, the Defense Department gave Foisie an award for meritorious service, ostensibly for serving briefly as ombudsman at *Stars and Stripes*, the armed services' daily.

To many of us at the *Herald Tribune*, there was something of the quiet American about the avuncular Phil. I write strictly of surmises—I wish to be perfectly clear on this point—but I confess mine were firmer than others' since I was able to watch the proceedings from the field. When Foisie appointed me to Hong Kong after my *Newsweek* calamity, I was one of the *Trib*'s first two correspondents in the region. My counterpart was yet another Australian, this one stationed in Singapore, who also wrote regularly for hawkish Australian defense magazines but infrequently and badly for us. No one in Paris said a word about my colleague's moonlighting, lax filing habits, and high school newspaper prose. When the subject arose in conversations with senior editors, as it did from time to time, I found the silence in combination with shrugs of resignation not quite eloquent but nearly.

I have only questions, but they accumulated during my years at the *Trib*. Reflecting on the paper's three Australian hires in Asia, peculiar at the very least, I cannot but ask whether the paper had longstanding, institutionalized ties to Western intelligence agencies vitally interested in the region. In an earlier time, would the *International Herald Tribune* have taken its place on that long list of corrupted publications Carl Bernstein compiled in the mid-seventies? Was Foisie in the file with Sulzberger, Paley, and the others, and if so, did the paper's connections survive him?

These questions beg two larger ones it is time to ask. Did the American press so compromise itself during the postwar decades that cooperation with intelligence is now among its permanent features? Have such arrangements been routinized? And then this, the biggest one: Have Americans lived in effect without an authentically independent press since 1945? We have only these imposing doubts. It is a pity even to entertain them, but we must. And so often, I have found, one's answers lie in one's questions.

THE TIMESIFICATION of the *International Herald Tribune* proceeded apace as I edited my excellent, competent, and objectionable correspondents. It was an unpleasant process to witness, the fates or worth of those affected never considered, but it was also interesting as a study providing I maintained my detachment. To watch New York take over the *Herald Trib* was to see the arrival of the new ideology of Jill Abramson's "patriotic journalism," as I will call it, ruin a newspaper that had until this time been indifferent to such notions and relatively untouched by them. Of a sudden there were *"Trib* people" and *"Times* people"—the phrases I used—and it was soon enough clear that the former were no longer welcome at the paper they had helped make what it was. Down-table copy editors would survive; the wire editor, a hire from Agence France-Presse, would stay on. But nobody at the top would. When my turn came, I greeted it with a silent sigh of relief. I had never wanted to command a newspaper's field brigade. Neither did I prove especially good at it under the circumstances Paris had handed me. My hours were long and exhausting: There was a flaw in the management design that the head office declined to address, and it left me overloaded. When Paris got around to replacing me, it gave two people the job I had done alone.

Neither did I want to resume work as a correspondent, but I agreed when the *Times*ified *Trib* suggested I serve as a kind of roving East Asia correspondent. I decided to make the best of it, though my alienation from the paper that had long been a professional home was by this time just short of complete. My first file would be a test of the waters. Would the *Herald Tribune* still publish the kind of work that had distinguished it among American-owned newspapers? It struck me as the right question at the right time.

Every story gets a "slug," one word to identify it throughout the editorial process, and I slugged this one DIPLOMACY. It was a long piece on the emergent influence of non-Western powers—China, India, and Russia in this case—and the implications of this for the global balance of power. Old dependencies were breaking, new alliances forming. Western markets would no longer be the only markets. By the middle of the new century's first decade, the United States had ceded control of many-sided talks on North Korea's nuclear question to China. Beijing, New Delhi, and Moscow were asserting their influence in the corresponding case of Iran's nuclear programs. These were my "hooks," non-Western solutions to non-Western problems. I think now it was by way of my reporting for this piece that I first recognized parity between West and non-West as a twenty-first century imperative, a theme I have often explored since.

Here are a few paragraphs from DIPLOMACY as filed in February 2006, lately discovered in the innards of an old computer:

> HONG KONG: The world's two pending nuclear crises, involving Iran and North Korea, are emerging as showcases for the rising diplomatic influence of China and India and a relative decline in that of America, according to senior officials, policymakers, and analysts in Asia and the United States....
>
> Washington had hoped to use improving relations with New Delhi to make it a loyal, across-the-board ally—not least as a balancing force against China. Instead, India has served notice that, from Nehru and the Non-Aligned Movement of the 1950s until its rise now as a diplomatic power, foreign policy remains a nonnegotiable emblem of its independence. India is now in a position to go from nonaligned to multi-aligned....
>
> The lasting lesson of North Korea and Iran, many officials and policy analysts say, is that the pillars of the Bush administration's foreign policy are becoming of less use. In neither case is military force a realistic option; in neither case do sanctions and isolation hold out much promise, and in both cases the international community plainly prefers the grays of diplomatic settlement to Washington's blacks and whites....

I knew well enough what I was doing. This was a thesis and a piece that reflected the *Herald Tribune* as it had been—worldly, balanced, its lens dilated. But it was not a piece you would be likely to find in *The Times*. It contradicted the orthodoxy, the narrative of American primacy—a highly sensitive matter since the 2001 events. I nickel-plated the file with this in mind. The reporting spanned ten days' interviewing with impeccable sources of various nationalities— Americans, Chinese, Indians, Iranians, South Koreans, Japanese. By the time I filed I could defend every syllable.

I will eat my hat or anything else suggested if the emergent world I identified in DIPLOMACY is not precisely the world we now see out our windows. You could see it then as easily as now, providing you insisted on seeing things as they were. But in my question, once again, lay my answer. Stories written beyond the ideological fence posts are never thrown back for that reason, as the fence posts cannot be acknowledged. It is always "We want better sourcing," or "Not enough solid reporting here," or the catch-all, "You don't support your case." My editor in Hong Kong hemmed and hawed before finally sending the piece on to Paris, whereupon more hemming and hawing ensued among top editors. The nervous uncertainty I detected among these colleagues amused and dismayed me all at once. As nobody could knock the piece over, it then went to New York, where a half-dozen *Times* correspondents and editors cast doubt on it, if vaguely. And at last, from my Hong Kong editor: "We just can't run it." This was the only explanation I ever got. "These people represent the upper echelons of American journalism," my editor added. He meant *Times* foreign-desk editors, bureau chiefs abroad, and a couple of national security reporters in especially good odor with management—all of whom missed the story, or simply could or would not write it, and consequently had conflicts of interest that glowed in the dark.

The upper echelons: I have ever since had a special affection for the phrase.

I read the fate of DIPLOMACY as warning, eight thousand miles' distant, of an advancing ideological conformity at *The New York Times* and, by extension, in American journalism. The *Times*ification of the *International Herald Tribune* seemed to me more, much more, than a publicly traded company absorbing an acquisition. The grip of orthodoxies, powerful for decades, had further tightened since I had left the States. There now seemed a subtly belligerent aggressiveness attaching to it. The post-2001 task, reflecting the insecure nation *The Times* wrote of and for, was to project outward from Eighth Avenue a global perspective now intolerant of any straying beyond the boundaries set by the national security state. Jingoism was no longer confined to its traditional quarters. It would be a few more years before the *International Herald Tribune* became the *International New York Times*. But the *Trib* was dead at the hands of clerks dedicated to pleasing a publisher long given to obliging powers other than the power the press ought to claim for itself. Decades before I picked up a pen and a notebook, Murrow had warned that American media were insulating readers and viewers from reality. With DIPLOMACY spiked, I had my second taste of the unbrave new world he described.

It was time for a stock-take, as there seemed nothing left worth doing at the *Herald Tribune*. "Never work for your newspaper," a colleague in Tokyo used to say. "Always make your newspaper work for you." This had struck me as cynical when I first heard it years earlier. Now I decided to try the advice. I did my best to honor the byline—it is on these that correspondents live or die—but I didn't honor it very often. Calibrating carefully, I filed as often as the worse of the two Australian correspondents—once a month or so. This period seems to me now a letter of resignation written over the course of a year.

I awakened before dawn one morning, unsure why, and sat by a window to watch the sun come up over the rooftops from my fifth-floor walkup. What occurred over that next hour or so seemed to come in a rush, a sudden epiphany. Floods of questions imposed themselves. How long did I propose to languish in private grief? What was I doing engaging in routine disagreements with editors when I was indifferent to their outcomes? Why had I been out of touch with my literary agent for two years? And above all: What did I propose to do with the years remaining to me, and what would I sacrifice to do it?

An extraordinary clarity and resolve came over me. To write honestly and more or less everything were my answers to those last two queries. In a matter of weeks I had a book synopsis on my agent's desk in New York, and in a matter of more weeks I was under contract with the editor, the late and missed Dan Frank at Pantheon, who I respected more than any other for his intellect, his craft, and for his insight— often better than mine—into what I was trying to do. Having signed off at last at the *International Herald* Tribune, I spent the next year reading, researching, and traveling, first through China, then India, and finally Japan. On my return to the cold-water flat in Elgin Street to get the writing done, I began lecturing at The University of Hong Kong, whose Journalism and Media Studies Centre, modeled after Columbia's graduate program, is universally held in high regard. It was on the Pok Fu Lam campus that I wrote and taught "Reinventing 'the Foreign Correspondent.'" I could not have wished for a better place to premiere the course. My students that first semester included mainland and local Chinese, an Indian, a Canadian, a Malaysian, a French Swiss, a Singaporean, a Dutchwoman, and two Americans. Their grasp of the imperative to transcend the Self and Other of the twentieth century, and all the other Cold War binaries, was intuitive.

Nothing that came to me during that exceptional dawn had come suddenly, in truth. That hour had been on its way for years. At some point previously, I had begun a farewell—several farewells, I think now—that extended far beyond the *Herald Tribune*'s newsroom. The book to come out of that time, *Somebody Else's Century: East and West in a Post–Western World*, was a gathering of thoughts accumulated over three decades as a correspondent and columnist. My graduate courses, especially "Reinventing," arose from those decades and were my best summations of the work needed to bring the craft into a new era. The most profound of these farewells was personal. I understood in the hour I describe that my years in corporate newspapers were over. I had no clear idea of what lay ahead. But my back had finally and fortunately been pushed against the wall. I knew, without putting it into words, that I would at last take full possession of that shadow I have mentioned previously, the who-I-truly-was as a professional and as a human being.

I learned a lesson during those first post-*Trib* years that has ever since stayed with me. This had to do with the rewards of modest living. My advance against royalties for *Century* had to cover a year's travel in China, India, and Japan—hotels, sustenance, trains, planes, interpreters—and then many months of writing. My faculty salary was more than a pittance but not by much. I wrote *Century* on a cutting board while sitting on the sofa in the Elgin Street flat, five storeys above a noisy bar district up from Victoria Harbor. Modest living began as a necessity. In time it became a preference, and then a pleasure. I also recognized it, in more time, as the doorway to good work. In simplicity lay freedom, I discovered a long time after Thoreau offered the advice.

It came time to go. The *Century* manuscript was with Dan Frank in New York. I had lectured for two years, and the household budget was critically depleted. Post-2001 America seemed to me the compelling topic, and what work lay ahead would lie there. For correspondents, returning home after a long time abroad is often difficult. All you have learned seems suddenly of little interest or use to others.

Those who have looked closely and paid attention have acquired a second pair of eyes, seeing as Americans see while seeing Americans as others see them. It can be a question of social alienation, of not fitting in, of having too few people to talk to. But I determined to make the transition, however hard it would prove.

The wonderfully vulgar Lyndon Johnson once observed that you are either inside the tent urinating out or outside the tent urinating in. It came to me in the weeks I spent packing that when I arrived home after many years, I would thenceforth stand outside the tent. And finally I understood, I remembered: This was where I had long earlier concluded it was best to be.

EVEN BEFORE I BOARDED a plane for that final flight home, as the spring of 2010 turned to summer, I had detected that Americans and many others concerning themselves with us were eager—indeed, on the way to desperate—for a new accounting of the United States and its place in the world. I heard this in conversations with Americans and non-Americans alike. I had seen it in the jubilation that greeted Barack Obama's election in the autumn of 2008, when the streets and bars in my neighborhood filled with celebrants. The invasion of Iraq had turned into a gruesome mess. The Pentagon had set the Middle East ablaze in the name of America the good, the peacemaker, the democratizer. Tensions with the Russian Federation were needlessly worsening. The first hints that the Obama presidency was to prove one of fraudulent promise were already evident. The old faith breaking, many minds yearned for a new story, a twenty-first century story that recorded the past as it was and so opened America to a different future. This story had not yet been written and was coming to seem long overdue.

For a brief time, it looked as though such a story would at last begin to be told. A couple of months before I arrived home, WikiLeaks released "Collateral Murder," the swiftly infamous video of a U.S. Army helicopter's attack on civilians in Baghdad. A month after my return came "Afghan War Diary," seventy-five thousand documents that devastated official accounts of America's post-2001 campaign in Afghanistan. Then came "Iraq War Logs" (392,000 Army field reports) and then "Cablegate," WikiLeaks' *coup de foudre* that eventful year, a collection of more than three million State Department email messages. WikiLeaks was all of four years old as it published these documents. Not since the Pentagon Papers thirty-nine years earlier had anyone penetrated so deeply into the recesses of Washington's culture of secrecy.

The moment seemed to conjure, at least in faint outline, that frisson of prideful determination Daniel Ellsberg's revelations had evoked among American journalists of the *[MORE]*-reading kind. In its early years WikiLeaks was understood to promise something new in journalism, a resource that would fundamentally alter relations between journalists and the powers they reported upon. *The New York Times* and other influential dailies embraced WikiLeaks and Julian Assange, its founder, republishing the 2010 releases with professional diligence. This suggested a reversal of the corrupt arrangements Jill Abramson described a short while later—a restoration of the press as an independent pole of power.

American media leapt before they looked that year, it seemed to me. They appeared not to recognize the choice they faced as they collaborated with WikiLeaks. Julian Assange and his organization were in the business of saying the unsayable, of bringing history to bear on events past and present. Sooner or later the American press would have to decide if this was at last its business, too.

If the press did not understand this choice at the time, the powers they covered—the Obama administration, the national security apparatus, the intelligence agencies—soon confronted them with it. Washington turned viciously against WikiLeaks after it released "Iraq War Logs," among the most damaging leaks in U.S. military history. It was quickly evident American media would dutifully follow. A concerted campaign to demonize Assange began at this time. The innovative colleague became the treasonous transgressor, the anti-American pariah, Assange who is a "Russian asset," Assange who is not a journalist. By the time the phased releases of "Cablegate" were coming out in the autumn of 2010, *The New York Times* was routinely conferring with the national security state as to what it would publish and what it would omit. It would do the same again when, three years later, Edward Snowden began to release the files he had copied from the National Security Agency's archives. In effect, those the press covered edited the publications covering them. I wish I could say with

confidence this must have marked a first in American journalism, but I
doubt it did. The practice has been business as usual from those years
onward.

To disclose, to reveal, to expose to public debate must count in
any serious definition of the press's responsibilities. It is by way of
these tasks that journalists take their place, an essential place, in public
space. Their rightful function is to serve as prompters in an inclusive
civic discourse. But with rare exceptions, American media had repu-
diated these responsibilities during the Cold War. And with the insti-
tutionalization of this abandonment after 2001, they became active
participants in what I judge to be an unprecedented sequestration of
power from public scrutiny and, hence, from democratic control. The
*arcana imperii* were more essential to the exercise of power now, and
there were multiples more of them. Protecting secrets counted among
the American press's perversely defined responsibilities by the time I
returned from Asia. I do not see that these assertions can be credibly
contested by journalists and apologists so deeply immersed in the
practices I describe as to be unable to recognize what they are doing.

Even before the 11 September attacks, Richard Perle, a longtime
presence in conservative circles, had given us the term "decontextual-
ization." Perle was on the Pentagon's Defense Policy Board in 2001,
and from this perch he marshaled his coinage on many occasions.
"We must decontextualize terrorism," Perle insisted. "Any attempt to
discuss the roots of terrorism is an attempt to justify it." I have to
count this among the stupider contentions I have ever been invited
to consider. Perle's intent was to counter those admirable many who
tried to open the 11 September tragedies to thoughtful questioning
as to history, causality, and responsibility. Who would have imagined
Perle's assertion, a retreat from reason itself, would define a soon-
to-be-prevalent practice among American media? In Hannah Arendt's
terms, Perle trafficked in "fragile facts." It is when acts of terrorism
are made to stand alone that they are most effectively deployed to
manipulate public opinion.

I have already noted the presence of POLO, the power of leaving
out, in the American press's Cold War repertoire. In the years since
2001, this practice, too, has been institutionalized. It is no longer a
question of what is erroneously missing in a news report. The omission of context is now a daily occurrence; no one in mainstream media

seems any longer to consider this a flaw. Omission—and it is time for someone in the profession to say this—is an insidious form of lying, akin to passive aggression, that most intractable of neuroses.

When Jill Abramson explained journalism's post-2001 relationship with power, she made one passing remark that is easily overlooked. The profession's incorporation of "national security" into its news judgments involved "a balancing test." If the government invoked national security in requesting that media censor themselves, this must be weighed against "our mandate to keep you all informed." Concern for national security seems typically to have gotten the higher mark in such tests, and it is beyond me how any journalist can accept this term without questioning it after all the decades of deceit and misconduct it has masked. Here I will consider the subtle but consequential assumption implicit in Abramson's description of the media's mandate. It takes its place in a discourse now a century old.

In 1920, the year he co-authored "A Test of the News," Walter Lippmann published the first of three books concerning the place of the press in a democratic society. *Liberty and the News* was followed in 1922 by *Public Opinion* and by *The Phantom Public* three years later. These books were progressively more pessimistic as to the ordinary citizen's capacity to understand a world that had grown more complex than any theretofore known.

Lippmann's reply to this, the coming of the modern in a mass society, was to preach the new gospel of the expert. He devised an interesting structure wherein experts were to deploy their expertise. They would have nothing to do with ordinary people and nothing to do with the making of official policy. With perfect disinterest, the expert advised the political class of scientifically determined realities, and out of this came correct policy, devoid of all special interest. The press's task in this schema was to convey these determinations to the public. In *Public Opinion*, Lippmann defined this duty as—famous phrase nowadays—"the manufacture of consent."

Here is Lippmann writing of "the private citizen" in *The Phantom Public*:

> Yet these public affairs are in no convincing way his affairs.
> They are managed, if they are managed at all, at distant
> centers, from behind the scenes, by unnamed powers.... He

lives in a world which he cannot see, does not understand and is unable to direct.

And, two chapters on in the same volume:

The actual governing is made up of a multitude of arrange-ments on specific questions by particular individuals. These rarely become visible to the private citizen. Government, in the long intervals between elections, is carried out by politicians, officeholders and influential men who make set-tlements with other politicians, officeholders and influential men. The mass of people see these settlements, judge them, and affect them only now and then. They are altogether too numerous, too complicated, too obscure in their effects to become the subject of any continuing exercise of public opinion.

Lippmann termed these severe judgments "democratic realism," though they seem to me neither democratic nor realistic. The press's place in this arrangement derived from Lippmann's idealization of invisible experts and those they advised. Journalists were to serve as adjuncts to the sequestered powers Lippmann described. They were to act as tribunes, in effect, handing down the decisions of these powers to all those incapable private citizens and cultivating public support for them. "The creation of consent is not a new art," he wrote in *Public Opinion*. "It is a very old one which was supposed to have died out with the appearance of democracy. But it has not died out. It has, in fact, improved enormously..."

John Dewey, the educationist and philosopher, reviewed the latter two books of Lippmann's triptych in *The New Republic* and published *The Public and Its Problems* in 1927. These amounted to replies to Lippmann's work. Dewey did not differ with Lippmann as to the citizen's limitations in a mass society, but he saw more democracy, not less, as the remedy. The judgments of the necessary elite, selected by virtue of class and privilege, must be subject to public deliberation, based on the public's understanding of all available perspectives on a given question. Setting out these perspectives was the press's true task. From this would emerge democratic consent or objection, and there would be no question of the press manufacturing it:

> It is not necessary that the many should have the knowledge and skill to carry on the needed investigations. What is required is that they have the ability to judge of the bearing of the knowledge supplied by others upon common concerns.

These indirect exchanges between two of the era's prominent thinkers come down to us as the "Lippmann-Dewey debate," although the two never engaged in one. While it is possible to exaggerate their differences, two are essential to grasp as we understand the press's failures since the Cold War, notably its deference to power in the post-2001 years. Lippmann encouraged the thought of the public as passive, the recipient of others' judgments. Citizens were bystanders—"spectators of action." Dewey saw the promise of participatory democracy even while he acknowledged the complexities of making it work. Nobody spectated, for politics was not spectacle; the civic self was reasserted, not extinguished. From this distinction arises a second, having to do with where journalists locate themselves in a democratic polity. Was it in the lofty towers above, as the messengers of those they report upon, or embedded in the citizens' midst, agents of an informed, infinitely sided public exchange? The question comes down to distance and proximity.

This is the divide, a very lopsided divide, that now defines American journalism. Jill Abramson, announcing "our mandate to keep you all informed," spoke the language of Lippmann. It is impossible to miss the presumption of remoteness from readers in these seven words. I doubt Abramson was aware that she had taken a position on a debate of critical importance to the profession—a problem of literacy, common among journalists. But she spoke for American media with this description of their task. In our time, mainstream media are densely populated with dedicated Lippmannites. I can think of no outstanding exception among corporate newspapers and broadcasters. Only of those media commonly called alternative can one say otherwise.

This is an especially perilous position for mainstream media to assume in the post-2001 context. It leaves them bound in complicity with the keepers of secrets, so assigning them the task of incessant omission in the news reports they bear downward to the public. I do not think it is in any wise a wonder that a markedly high proportion of our "private citizens" now distrust mainstream media, in large measure, we can safely surmise, because of these lies of omission and of secrets withheld. Pew Research, Gallup, and other polling organizations have been measuring public sentiment on this question for many years. Gallup, in an iteration of its "Confidence in Institutions" survey published in the summer of 2022, found that 16 percent of those surveyed trust what they read in American newspapers; 11 percent of Americans trust broadcasters of television news to give them full and accurate accounts of events. I read this stunningly widespread dissatisfaction as altogether healthy. It seems to me one measure of Americans' discernible desire to see the world as it is, not as anyone wishes it to be—to begin to write, this is to say, a new story, a new narrative, a new metanarrative, or whatever we wish to call it.

And it is ever clearer as the years go by: There will be no new American story from our corporate newspapers and broadcasters, however pressing the need, so long as they situate themselves as appendages of power in Lippmannite fashion. The old story, the mythical story, the seventeenth-century, history-is-elsewhere story finally failed at the start of our century. But this story will nonetheless be told and told again, a forlorn effort to hold history at bay, condemning us to an eternal present wherein no alternative future can be imagined. This leaves many Americans, too many, in a state of psychological turmoil that may have no precedent in our history.

"In an ever-changing, incomprehensible world the masses had reached the point where they would, at the same time, believe everything and nothing, think that everything was possible and that nothing was true," Hannah Arendt wrote in a memorable passage in *The Origins of Totalitarianism*. "Mass propaganda discovered that its audience was ready at all times to believe the worst, no matter how absurd, and did not particularly object to being deceived because it held every statement to be a lie anyhow."

Arendt was looking back to the Nazi regime and Stalin's Soviet Union when she wrote her celebrated 1951 treatise. But the thought seems never to have been thereafter far from her mind. In a conversation with a French free-speech activist not long before her death in 1975, Arendt had yet blunter words as to what eventually comes of circumstances such as ours. "If everybody always lies to you," she said to Roger Errera, "the consequence is not that you believe the lies, but rather that nobody believes anything any longer."

# 4.

# Toward an Authentic Journalism.

> But the utility of intelligence is admitted
> only theoretically, not practically; it is not
> desired that ordinary people should think
> for themselves, because it is felt that people
> who think for themselves are awkward to
> manage and cause administrative problems.
>
> ———Bertrand Russell,
> "Free Thought and
> Official Propaganda,"
> 1922.

I BEGAN ANOTHER BOOK after arriving home from the East
in mid-2010. In it I made the case that Americans were ready for
that new story I sensed they had begun to look for after the events of
2001. Myth, to put this point another way, was giving way to history:
This was my most essential observation. In the spring of 2013, Yale
University Press brought out *Time No Longer: Americans After the
American Century*. It was my first book dedicated to my own country—its predicaments, its opportunities, its choices.

Shortly after publication, Yale's publicity director telephoned
with news that *Salon* had acquired rights to run an extract in its
Memorial Day editions. Dave Daley, *Salon*'s editor at the time, settled
on a section having to do with how America's idea of itself was fated
to change in the twenty-first century. I thought this an astute choice.
The response from readers in the comment thread was lively—another

confirmation of what I had begun to detect from the other end of the Pacific.

*Salon* intrigued me. Here was an online journal that published my thoughts on America's propelling myths—a topic that would never have found a place in corporate media. I called Daley to ask if we could meet. When we had coffee somewhere in the West Thirties a few days later we agreed to revive my foreign affairs column, which hadn't had a home in some years. The money shocked me: After haggling awkwardly, I got Daley up to a hundred fifty dollars a column. Adjusted for inflation, my weekly salary at the *Guardian* four decades earlier was three times that. I decided to give it a year. Another door seemed to stand slightly ajar.

The summer of 2013 turned out to be the liveliest of seasons. In June Edward Snowden, the former NSA contractor, began revealing the agency's extravagant global surveillance programs. A month later came the U.S.-authorized coup in Cairo that brought down the elected government of Mohamed Morsi. In mid-August news broke of a chemical-weapons attack in a suburb of Damascus, the Syrian capital, bringing the Obama administration to the brink of a missile assault on the Assad government. In September, good news at last: Hassan Rouhani, Iran's just-elected president, electrified the U.N. General Assembly when he extended the hand of reconciliation and opened the way to talks governing the Islamic Republic's nuclear programs.

I watched and wrote all summer and into the autumn. I was new to digital publishing, and in retrospect late. Like others who had come up and worked in print journalism, internet publications did not at first seem altogether as serious. There was no smell of ink, nothing to hold in your hands. This mistaken judgment had the benefit of setting me free. It allowed me to let myself go in the columns. My language loosened from the formalities of *Herald Tribune* English, mainstream media English. If I didn't go in search of a new voice, a new voice found me. It was more authentically mine than any to which I had grown accustomed. With it I addressed readers more directly than I previously had. Without quite understanding what had happened, I had removed some barrier of convention, of decorum, that separates journalists from readers as a proscenium distances stage actors from audiences. I wrote in another register now, using an other-than-approved vocabulary that kept the columns closer to the truth of things, and closer to readers, than most of what you could read in the mainstream dailies.

There was no writing honestly about foreign affairs anymore without making oneself a media critic. Foreign coverage had been poor in my younger years and was often poorer during my decades in Asia. Now it was the worst in my lifetime and was deteriorating further, it seemed, by the day. Omission, mis-, and disinformation were common topics in my commentaries. Washington's authorization of the Egyptian coup, via Susan Rice, Barack Obama's national security adviser, was mentioned once in mainstream press reports, by David Kirkpatrick and Mayy El Shiekh in *The New York Times*, and evidently by accident, for this momentous fact ever after disappeared. The murderous jihadists the United States was covertly funding, arming, and training in Syria were routinely misidentified as "moderate rebels"—a now-infamous instance of willful falsification. That August 2013 gas attack outside Damascus was patently a provocation arranged by these same jihadists to draw U.S. forces directly into the war, as Seymour Hersh later established in the *London Review of Books*. To this day the incident is misreported as Bashar al-Assad's grim work against his own people. These were among the more prominent of numerous cases of deliberate distortion and defactualization as I revived my column in *Salon*.

Jacques Ellul, the Christian anarchist and many-sided intellectual, thought propaganda the gravest danger facing advanced societies because it is most powerful when used to manipulate domestic audiences: If its object is the control of perception and thought, it is the aspirations, drives, and fears of the individual that the propagandist must understand most thoroughly. "Effective propaganda can work only inside a group, principally inside a nation," Ellul tells us in the study he titled *Propaganda*. We must weigh the thought carefully. American media's latest descent into the base practice of propaganda occurred at a particular time—post-2001 time, I will call it. If the events of that year threatened America's identity, our consciousness of ourselves as exceptional, the project in the years since has been the preservation of America's self-image—that value Hannah Arendt and Daniel Boorstin had identified at roughly the same time. Ellul's subtitle is *The Formation of Men's Attitudes*. This described corporate media's pressing task by the time I started publishing in *Salon*. Washington's defense of empire had become more aggressive, more visible, and more censurable—all of these while there was supposed to be no such thing. America's repeated abuses of international law, its aggressions across the Middle East, the suffering inflicted on Iranians, Syrians, Libyans, Venezuelans, and others: All of this was blurred or kept from public view altogether so as to preserve Americans' light-of-the-world idea of themselves. The conduct of empire requires domestic consensus—or at least acquiescence. Accounts of events that left us to our own "attitudes" would no longer do. We had to be "encircled," to take Ellul's evocative term. "Propaganda," Edward Bernays wrote in his 1928 work on the topic, "is the executive arm of the invisible government." This is what the American press had made of itself by the second decade of our century, behind pretenses to independence even thinner than they had been during the Cold War decades.

I had pushed Dave Daley up to two hundred dollars a column as my readership grew, but it was difficult to keep on. It was a turn in my thinking that sustained me. Forty years earlier, when I was editing the foreign report at the *Guardian*, I had determined to train myself in the mainstream press's disciplines, in time achieving mastery to the extent I was capable of it. The time would come, so I imagined, when I could apply this acquired craft to a sustaining, authentically independent press. A recognition now came gradually. The professional standards were not as I had hoped. The writing and editing were often poor. There was no dusty loft off Union Square and little common purpose as we had during the antiwar years. All this was so different that I hadn't noticed where I stood. It was at the threshold of the door *Salon* had held open to me. To pass through it would be to approach that place I had long earlier set out to find.

It had arrived differently than I had thought it would, it did not look as I had anticipated, I could not have imagined the technologies wherein it thrived, but there was an independent press to publish work such as mine, just as I had long earlier hoped there would be. These media are sites of wholeness, I will call them, where journalists can reclaim their integrated selves, make themselves one with their shadows as I have used this term. I count this among their most essential and powerful features. I look to them now for the future of the profession I chose those many years back.

"THE INFORMATION AGE is actually a media age. We have war by media, censorship by media, demonology by media, retribution by media, diversion by media—a Surreal assembly line of obedient clichés and false assumptions."

That is John Pilger, the Australian-British journalist and film-maker, lecturing at the University of California, Berkeley, in December 2014. He spoke of Western media's "power to create a new 'reality.'" He spoke of their "critical role in conditioning their readers to accept a new and dangerous cold war." He quoted a British official explaining how media disseminated the Foreign Office's deceptions: "We would feed journalists factoids of sanitized intelligence, or we would freeze them out." This was the access game. All that the British do in this line, I should note, they either taught the Americans or learned from them.

Eleven months before Pilger spoke in Berkeley, demonstrations in Kiev tipped over into a violent coup that forced Ukraine's elected president, Viktor Yanukovych, into exile. Ukraine had long been part of Washington's design to encircle the Russian Federation. By February 2014 the policy cliques had determined it was time to move decisively. American support for the putschists, who included professed neo-Nazi militias, is a matter of record—even if it now requires some effort to find the record. Moscow's subsequent move to secure its southwestern border and the Crimean Peninsula, location of its only warm-water port, was a response an undergraduate in politics could anticipate. This is also true of the eight years that ensued, during which Kiev incessantly shelled the Russian-speaking population in Ukraine's eastern provinces, and of the war that followed those years in consequence of NATO's insistent advance eastward to the Russian frontier. I am well aware that these matters are even now disputed. This reflects the exceptional extent to which a perfectly legible body of evidence has been obscured.

There is no way to describe the mainstream American press coverage of these events as other than purposeful propaganda. It made no reference to the U.S. role in cultivating the Kiev coup, no mention of Washington's strategic plans and Ukraine's place in them. Many newspapers reported the prominence of neo-Nazis in Kiev, clearly if rarely. Once Russia intervened militarily in February 2022, these same newspapers and their sources denied the existence of the extremists. Only in so-called alternative media or in some non-American publications did one read of any of these things. This was a case of POLO, the power of leaving out, on a grand scale, disturbing most of all because it proved so effective. All suggestion of cause and effect was erased. Pilger put it best when he addressed his audience in Berkeley: "The suppression of the truth about Ukraine is one of the most complete news blackouts I can remember."

A crisis in Syria had also unfolded by the time Pilger spoke, and I am confident it informed his thinking. A long war began as the Ukraine coup would a little later, with legitimate demonstrations against the sitting government. They started in 2011, roughly speaking a Syrian rendering of the Arab Spring. But what followed was never a civil war, as the press named it. By early 2012 at the latest, the United States had turned the early protests into another coup operation, as it armed and financed Sunni extremists who included al-Qaeda, its various offshoots, and in time the Islamic State. This will appear shocking only to those who do not know their history. The Syria operation was a straight reprise of the Afghanistan strategy Zbigniew Brzezinski, as Jimmy Carter's national security adviser, sold his president in late 1979: Train, bankroll, and arm the enemy of America's enemy and never mind its fanatical tendencies. In the Afghanistan case the objective was to mire the Soviets in a mess; in Syria it was to bring down a government that resisted Washington's imperial pretensions and had longstanding relations with Russia.

Many readers found it difficult to accept these realities, so wholly did Washington's accounts of events contradict them. But the evidence, the documents, the testimonies, the records—these are all there. It eventually came to light that the State Department, the CIA, the British Foreign Office, and various organizations they support had conducted expensive disinformation campaigns that successfully manipulated Syria coverage at *The New York Times*, the other major dailies, the wire services, and the major broadcasters. Documents leaked from the Foreign Office in September 2020 revealed the extraordinary extent of this operation. Local journalists were trained and co-opted in large numbers, more than fifteen hundred Western journalists were cultivated to reproduce planted news stories, public-relations contractors were engaged to rebrand murderous Salafists as democracy-loving idealists. The Foreign Office leak was never reported in mainstream publications: The documents were exposed by *The Grayzone*, one of our more enterprising independent publications. Here we come to a nearly intractable problem that has its amusing side: Most people who rely on corporate media seem to assume that if a propaganda program of this magnitude were in train they would read about it in their newspapers.

In May 2016, *The New York Times Magazine* published a piece of exceptionally revealing journalism, a rare and remarkable work for its bold forthrightness. It was a lengthy profile of Ben Rhodes by a reporter named David Samuels. Rhodes was an aspiring fiction writer when, by the unlikeliest of turns, he found his way into the inner circle of the Obama White House as deputy national security adviser for strategic communications. His job was to sell foreign policy to the American public. It was to spin "some larger restructuring of the American narrative," as Samuels put it. "Rhodes is a storyteller who uses a writer's tools to advance an agenda that is packaged as politics."

Rhodes and Ned Price, his deputy, were social-media acrobats. Price, a former CIA analyst and at writing the State Department's spokesman, recounted without inhibition how he fed White House correspondents, columnists, and others in positions to influence public opinion as a *foie gras* farmer feeds his geese. Here is Price on the day-to-day of the exercise:

> There are sort of these force multipliers. We have our *compadres*. I will reach out to a couple of people, and, you know, I wouldn't want to name them. … And I'll give them some color, and the next thing I know, lots of these guys are in the dot-com publishing space and have huge followings, and they'll be putting out this message on their own.

Rhodes gives Samuels a more structured analysis of this arrangement:

> All the newspapers used to have foreign bureaus. Now they don't. They call us to explain to them what is happening in Moscow or Cairo. Most of the outlets are reporting on world events from Washington. The average reporter we talk to is 27 years old, and their only reporting experience consists of being around political campaigns. That's a sea change. They literally know nothing.

I wrote a lengthy *Salon* column on *The Times* piece. Rhodes and Price were describing the descendants of Jill Abramson and her cohort. Some qualitative difference in the press's relations with power had then been set in motion. There were earlier indications of things to come—as early as the mid–Cold War years, indeed—but American media's Lippmannite subservience to the national security state was now seamlessly consolidated. Journalists no longer needed to understand the events they reported upon, the accounts of never-named government officials could be reported as fact, and one side of a story was enough so long as it was the American side. "When you read routine press reports in *The Times* or any of the other major dailies," I wrote of the Rhodes profile, "you are looking at what the clerks we still call reporters post on government bulletin boards (which we still call newspapers)." The press, in other words, had reached the point it was altogether dependent on the geese-feeding arrangement when it reported on national security questions. The record since does nothing to contradict this conclusion. The record does a great deal, indeed, to support it.

IN MID-JULY 2016, WikiLeaks published nearly twenty thousand email messages pilfered from the Democratic National Committee's computer system. The release was acutely embarrassing, providing evidence that the DNC had subverted the political campaign of Bernie Sanders, a social democrat, in favor of Hillary Clinton's as they competed to run later that year against Donald Trump. WikiLeaks published the stolen mail on Friday, 22 July. Within two days, Clinton campaign officials began asserting that "the Russians" had hacked the DNC's mail "for the purpose of helping Donald Trump." I have quoted Robby Mook, Clinton's campaign manager. On back-to-back Sunday morning news programs, Mook cited "experts" he never named and evidence neither he nor anyone else ever presented, described, or explained. American media, as if reading cues, ignored the damaging contents of the stolen mail to focus their reporting on the purported Russian hack as if it were proven fact. By the time Trump carried the election in November 2016, the Democrats and the media were extravagantly overinvested in a narrative they would have to sustain at least through the new president's first term. So did work begin on the built-on-sand edifice known as Russiagate.

The press fell into a feverish delirium once Trump won the 2016 election, and the Russiagate story thereafter grew to astonishing proportions. President Trump, members of his family, and various people around him stood accused of extensive collusion with Russians. A half-dozen simultaneous investigations proceeded into these matters. Robert Mueller, a former director of the Federal Bureau of Investigation, was named special counsel and convened a grand jury. Allegations of treason were many; prominent political figures and many media cultivated a case for impeachment. Trump's presidency was in many respects crippled from the start. Those few of his ideas one could count sound—a new détente with Russia, a reduced military presence abroad, an end to foreign wars of adventure, a negotiated settlement with North Korea, the easing of NATO into the history books—got nowhere. None of the allegations leveled at Trump and his administration, and a great many more aimed elsewhere, were substantiated, but all of them were reported as factually so at one time or another, in one newspaper or another, by one or another broadcaster. These reports relied almost invariably on the word of unnamed intelligence officials—word then advanced as evidence.

The Russiagate narrative grew top-heavy as its elaborations accumulated over the course of several years. These were cruel, messy years. Journalists who questioned the orthodox version of events had their work rejected or were "canceled"—depressing echoes of the Cold War decades. I had my own bitter taste of this drift back into irrationality. I had moved my column to *The Nation* by the time Russiagate was in full flower. In August 2017 I reported on the first reliable evidence, based on forensic science and gathered by a group of dissident intelligence professionals, that neither the Russians nor anyone else could have compromised the DNC's computers remotely. The speed of the download indicated the theft had to have been executed by someone with direct access to the equipment. It was an inside job—a leak, not a hack. By this time *The Nation*'s editors had turned the magazine into a grotesque, upside-down mirror of its long and honorable history as an independent weekly with no debts or ties to vested interests, political or otherwise. Its newsroom, staffed with "leftists," "progressives" (quotation marks required), and assorted ideologues obsessed with Hillary Clinton's downfall and Trump's rise, erupted in a juvenile frenzy after the column was published. The piece has never been substantively discredited, but I was fired a short time later—the Klieg lights, once again, having gone off.

The Russiagate story eventually collapsed of its own weight, as did the many allegations associated with it. The Mueller investigation, the equivalent of the Church Committee for its prominence, came up with nothing on the collusion question. Many prominent Democrats and national security officials who had professed in front of micro-phones and cameras to have or have seen evidence of Russia's malev-olent deeds admitted in Senate testimonies they had none and had seen none. This was in May 2017. Crowdstrike, the cybersecurity firm that claimed to have forensic data establishing the Russian hack of the DNC's mail, similarly acknowledged it had no such data. What a difference a legally binding oath seemed to make. At the insistence of Capitol Hill Democrats, these admissions of duplicity were not made public for three years. You would have thought the mainstream press would have covered the May 2017 testimonies, momentous as they were, when they were at last disclosed in April 2020. But no major newspaper or broadcaster has ever reported them. Nor has *The Nation*, I will add. Mainstream and liberal American media simply stopped reporting the Russiagate story as it fell apart.

In January 2023, Jeff Gerth, an investigative journalist of excellent reputation, published a four-part series in the *Columbia Journalism Review* that prompts me to think of him as the Stuart Loory of our time. In more than 24,000 words rendered in exceptional detail, Gerth exposed more or less all of American media's craven complicity in manufacturing out of nothing all the fabrications as to Donald Trump's collusion with Russia as he ran against Hillary Clinton in the 2016 presidential election. As Loory had done in 1973, when he exposed the press's covert collaborations with the CIA, Gerth lifted the lid on publishers, editors, and reporters who knowingly lied, left unsaid, dis-informed, and covered up the Democratic Party's campaign to smear Clinton's opponent and then cripple Donald Trump's presidency. The postscript to Gerth's report is to me as disheartening as the piece itself. In the course of his reporting Gerth asked 60 journalists with unclean hands for comment. A minority responded; none accepted his or her culpability. No major publication or broadcaster Gerth approached replied to his questions during his investigation. It was "no comment" straight down the line. Even with American media's Cold War history to hand, their refusal to acknowledge their irresponsible conduct during the Russiagate affair must still count as breathtaking.

As Edward Murrow suggested in another context long ago, at this point we must leave it to the historians to untangle the intricate web woven to undermine Trump the candidate and Trump our forty-fifth president. I am interested here in the disfiguring scars the Russiagate episode has etched onto the American body politic. These are evident in the gravely worsened condition of corporate media, certainly. But the damage the press sustained, mostly self-inflicted, cannot be separated from what American media's fraudulent Russiagate coverage has done to close American minds, to discourage independent thought, to foreclose on open, rational, democratic debate. In all of this the most enduring effects of Russiagate may prove to be psychological, just as the Cold War had a psychological dimension not often considered.

A congeries of interests, each with its own motives, lay behind the Russiagate ruse. The national security apparatus and the military were alarmed by Trump's foreign policy platform. These constituencies appear to have had little difficulty recruiting the Obama Justice Department and the FBI to the anti-Trump cause. The Democratic leadership, after its mail was leaked and published, found it useful to promote the Russiagate narrative as a compelling vilification of a political opponent and a distraction from the party's internal corruption. The press and broadcasters acted in concert with these interests, having long supported America's militarized foreign policy and the Democrats' version of the liberal world order. The consolidation of this four-sided alliance should worry all of us for its power and totality. As a threat to what remains of American democracy it is altogether worthy of the term "Deep State," which, hardly a coincidence in my view, appeared in the national discourse during the time I describe.

As the Russiagate narrative grew to its implausible proportions, mainstream media resorted to one of the most insidious propaganda techniques at their disposal. Psychologists at Villanova and Temple universities identified the illusory truth effect, or reiteration effect, in experiments conducted during the late nineteen seventies: Repeat obvious fallacies often enough and even rational minds will take them to be true. We live with this daily now. I watch in wonder as the process unfolds regularly in *The Times* and elsewhere. What is first reported as "alleged" or "possible" or "suspected" subsequently becomes "likely" or "probable" on its way to assuming the solidity of truth. Verbs make the same journey, the conditional—"might," "could," "may have"— moving onto the certainty of "was," or "did," or "is." During my *Salon* years I took to timing this practice: It generally spans two to three weeks, although it sometimes proceeds much more swiftly. Anyone with the patience to do so can follow this phenomenon in the archives of *The Times* or any of the other major dailies or broadcast networks.

Maybe with intent and maybe not, Russiagate's promoters, not least the press, tipped the nation into one of those periodic bouts of hysteria that have been a feature of the American story since the seventeenth-century Quaker hangings in Boston. By the time Trump was voted out of office we were face to face with the illiberality that, as de Tocqueville observed and as Henry Steele Commager and other distinguished historians have since addressed, has always lain at the heart of American liberalism. Trump is gone now, at this writing maybe for good, but the ever-more-manifest imperative to conform to the dictates of the righteous majority—the "soft despotism" de Tocqueville identified a hundred and ninety years ago—is now a potent feature of our political culture, perfectly evident in the spirit of intolerance abroad among us.

As previously suggested, I trace the press's malpractice and the more profound societal crisis I describe to the events of 2001 and the loss of faith that followed. American institutions have steadily weakened since then. Forms, procedures, routines, norms: These remain. But the poor judgment and often the irresponsibility and misconduct of those charged with leading and administering the American polity, and I include here the press, have hollowed out these institutions, procedures, and norms. The spirit that once inspired their creation and observance seems to have deadened. In its place, as I read the case, some peculiar need to submit to institutional authority, even when this means ignoring long records of falsification, appears to have overtaken many Americans, very possibly a majority.

All that we now file under "Russiagate," to put the point another way, has left Americans a people decisively, palpably adrift. They appear to nurse a never-spoken fear—rightfully, I think—that they are nearer the abyss of a failed "American experiment" than they ever thought they would be. They are left to turn to the very people and institutions that have betrayed them out of sheer want of some alternative structure in which they can still invest belief. At this stage in the long story of the American press since the Cold War, I fault it for making cynical use of this prevalent condition.

H ENRY LUCE, PUBLISHER of *TIME, LIFE,* and *Fortune,* at one time owner of the ABC broadcasting network and various other media properties, seems to have been a worried man in 1942. The American press was by this time well along in its transformation into what it is now: a highly concentrated, corporate-owned business well aware of its power but without a great deal of regard for its duties as a civic institution in public space. The Great Depression had brought Americans to a degree of political awareness it is difficult now to imagine. The reading and listening public was, no surprise, highly suspicious of the use corporatized media made of their accumulating influence. Major publishers and broadcasters—Luce, the Cowles family, the Radio Corporation of America (a subsidiary of General Electric with close ties to government and the military)—did not enjoy great popularity. The press and broadcasters were not, by and large, trusted institutions.

"Crisis" may not be too strong a term for these circumstances, just as it is not now. Luce, who had a year earlier declared "the American century" in a famous *LIFE* editorial, had great aspirations for the land of the free. His response to Americans' deep and broad resentment of the press was to ask Robert Hutchins, president of the University of Chicago, to convene a commission to look into things. Luce wrote a check for two hundred thousand dollars, roughly three and a half million dollars today, and Hutchins chose, with Luce approving, thirteen prominent names, among them Reinhold Niebuhr, Arthur Schlesinger, Harold Lasswell, and Archibald MacLeish. The Hutchins Commission met periodically over four years and published *A Free and Responsible Press* in 1947. We must note the date if we are to understand this document in the context of the Cold War's enduring effects on American journalism. As mentioned in an earlier chapter, it was understood by 1947 that public opinion would have to be manipulated ever more thoroughly. The press, it hardly bears mentioning, was essential to this undertaking.

Hutchins wanted no journalists on the commission, and Luce acquiesced when Hutchins named none. Neither was interested in hearing from journalists about what ailed journalism, we can fairly assume. That was not at bottom their topic: Public attitudes were their topic. The project was to enlist the press in making America the kind of America that would befit a century Luce had named after it—an exceptional America, a powerful America, a capitalist America, a corporatized America, an ideologically driven America. The title of the Hutchins Commission's report bears scrutiny. The only serious threats to a free press in America at this time were the ownership structure Luce exemplified and the press's willing support of the Cold War cause. The operative term was "responsible," as in this passage, from page twenty-seven of the first edition:

> We must recognize, however, that the agencies of mass communication are an educational instrument, perhaps the most powerful there is; they must assume a responsibility like that of educators in stating and clarifying the ideals toward which the community should strive.

"What kind of society do we want? What do we have? How can the press be used ... to get what we want?" These were the questions Hutchins charged the commission's members with answering.

We read here of the improper instrumentalization of the press— the perversion of its purpose. It is not the press's responsibility to tell society what its ideals are: These are for society to decide by way of open debate of the sort Dewey urged. The same is to be said in the matter of determining the kind of society Americans should wish to live in. "How can we use the press to get what we want?" Who is the "we" in this question, and who licenses this "we" to use the press to their ends? *A Free and Responsible Press* is replete with rhetoric of this kind, augustly rendered prose in favor of turning the press into the propaganda machine required to reverse the ideals of Roosevelt's New Deal and, by 1947, to wage the Cold War.

It is remarkable how little has changed since the publication of *A Free and Responsible Press*. The corporate press and broadcasters still wonder why so many Americans, and for nearly twenty years now a majority, neither like them nor trust them. As I noted earlier, the size of this majority has grown to astonishing proportions. Media still grapple, or purport to, with the problems the Hutchins Commission took up, or purported to take up. Committees inquire, symposia analyze, columnists and editors ruminate on the mystery of it all. What is wrong and how can we fix it? Three-quarters of a century later, it is the same question: How can we make Americans accept what we tell them as to the kind of society they should want America to be?

"Today those complexities have deepened," Michael Luo noted in a July 2020 *New Yorker* piece summoning the Luce-Hutchins project. "And yet the work of the Hutchins Commission remains a touchstone, in part because of the way it lays out the virtues to which journalism can aspire in a democracy." The naïveté of this reading is symptomatic of the intellectual underdevelopment of Luo's cohort of journalists. It is preposterous to suggest that what the Hutchins Commission urged on the press had anything to do with "virtue." The Hutchins group pretended to diligent examination of American media's malaise but concluded that the press needed simply to make more rigorous efforts to persuade Americans of "the ideals toward which the community should strive"—ideals as determined by the various elites for whom Luce, Hutchins, and their congress of the wise spoke. The implicit thought in 1947 was that to address the divide between the press and its public it was the latter that needed remedial work. Those fretting today about media's loss of credibility presume the same. *It is not us. We are trustworthy, responsible, and good at what we do. It is our readers and viewers who must be brought around.*

IN AUGUST 2016, a month after Donald Trump won the Republican nomination, *The New York Times's* media reporter declared on page one that the paper would no longer observe customary professional standards in its coverage of Trump the presidential contender. "Trump Is Testing the Norms of Objectivity in Journalism" was the headline atop Jim Rutenberg's piece. "Let's face it," he wrote. "Balance has been on vacation since Mr. Trump stepped onto his golden Trump Tower escalator last year to announce his candidacy."

I give full credit to *The Times* for its honesty in this case. Its reporting on Trump the candidate and Trump the forty-fifth president was from the outset an unbecoming dishonor to the profession. Little the paper published about Trump and his administration was without its anti-Trump bias, implicit or explicit depending on the case. Discarding a century of history, *The Times* reported as if it were Trump alone who entertained relations with right-wing dictators. Trump's summits and telephone calls with Vladimir Putin were betrayals bordering on treason, and let the ordinary protocols of statecraft go unmentioned. One need not hold Trump in high regard to observe this framework of deceit as *The Times* constructed and elaborated it, often by keeping its readers well clear of context. The essential points here are simply stated. We could not trust *The New York Times*'s reporting on Donald Trump: The paper told us so. As our polity fractured more profoundly than at any time at least since the Vietnam War, the once-but-no-longer newspaper of record intended not to report this critical turn professionally but to take a side in it—the side of the national security state and those in the Democratic Party who speak for it in the political sphere. *The Times* told us this, too.

Objectivity has been a contentious question for journalists since it was elevated to a professional orthodoxy a century ago. Let us define it as the notion of truth untouched by opinion, sentiment, bias, belief, or ideology. Or: principled, disinterested fidelity to available evidence, all of it, even when it may conflict with one's perspectives and leanings. Walter Lippmann was among objectivity's influential advocates in the nineteen twenties, but there began the complications. Objectivity was soon put to other uses: Newspapers and radio broadcasters that were other than objective cited their objectivity to claim elevated authority over their audiences. Publishers and editors, as earlier recounted, used the imperative of objectivity to straitjacket reporters and neuter their faculties of discernment and judgment. The intent was to naturalize, to borrow Nancy Bernhard's term again, prevalent ideologies and orthodoxies—American exceptionalism, pre–Cold War anti-Communism, what we now call free-market fundamentalism. These were advanced as objective realities in no need of critical inspection.

Journalists of the kind who read *[MORE]* in the 1970s were right to hold the encrusted dogma of objectivity up to the light. They did so in the name of the uncorrupted ideal. This is the ideal of objective reason, which dates to the ancient Greeks. It requires that thought be conducted without reference to the desirability or otherwise of its conclusions. To make any such reference is to succumb to subjective reason. Socrates taught us that reason should determine belief: To allow belief to determine reason is the danger implicit in subjective reason. The late Robert Parry, a journalist of impeccable integrity, put the case for objective reason this way: "I don't care what the truth is. I just care what the truth is."

Ideals are never fully realized: This is so by definition, and certainly it holds for journalists. But ideals are to be striven for nonetheless. And it is every journalist's duty, no less, to do this striving toward the ideal of objectivity. From the moment an editor or reporter decides on which story to cover and which to leave alone, personal judgments and all that inform them are at work. There is nothing to be done about this and only one sound way for journalists to think about it. This requires an understanding of one's responsibilities, quite special responsibilities, and the discipline to honor them. This was the point back in the *[MORE]* days, when conscientious journalists challenged the misuse of the principle of objectivity. It is among the lessons I learned when corresponding from Portugal very early in my professional years.

Now objectivity is up for consideration once again. But the project is not to restore the ideal: As *The New York Times* indicated at the time of Trump's political ascendancy, it is to discard the ideal altogether. The triumph of subjective reason, wherein thought is assigned the purpose of producing a desired outcome, has been a long time coming. Max Horkheimer identified this as among the maladies of our time—"the sickness of the thinking mechanism"—in the book I cited earlier, *The Eclipse of Reason*, which he published, it is worth noting, the same year the Hutchins Commission brought out its report.

"'Objectivity' has lost its usefulness as a shorthand for journalism's aspirations," Michael Luo suggested in his 2020 *New Yorker* piece. At the time, a reporter for one of the networks dismissed objectivity as "a failed experiment." Reading these and other commentaries like them gives the strong impression that journalists active today in the mainstream press are well on the way to making a mess of the matter, if they have not landed themselves in one already. Their thoughts as to what ought to replace the ideal of objectivity amount to a case for radical subjectivity, for a license to infuse one's work with all that was previously to be guarded against: belief, emotion, bias, ideology. Wesley Lowery, who rendered the "failed experiment" judgment, calls this "moral clarity" but fails to explain whose morality he means. Lippmann lives in phrases such as Lowery's.

Not to be missed in all of this, the subjectivists, as I will call them, wrap their biases and beliefs in the very language of those they purport to oppose—the traditional language of objectivity. It is in this way the subjectivists take us straight back to Lippmann and the restoration of objectivity-as-pose. With the history of this question in view I can think of few greater ironies. But a reading of any major daily's front page on any given day makes this point quite clearly: We find the same sonorous, authoritative diction and the same faux disinterest used to naturalize contempt for whomever or whatever the press wants to attack and approval of whatever it wishes to favor. It is by way of this professional sleight of hand that advocates of subjectivity propose to naturalize their ideological proclivities as none other than objective truth. Executive editors and senior broadcast executives who ought to know better now stamp their approval on this travesty. We have returned to the nineteen twenties.

This is what I mean by a mess: I mean a professional, ethical, and moral mess. If we could not rely on the corporate press and broadcasters as they covered Donald Trump or some other figure not to their liking, shall we assume they are truthfully and impartially covering anything or anybody else? Relations with Russia and China? Crises in such places as Syria and Ukraine? Russiagate, indeed?

SHORTLY AFTER DONALD TRUMP was elected president, a group journalists and national security officials published *PropOrNot*, a list of two hundred publications it declared to be organs of Russian propaganda. *Consortium News*, where my columns at this writing appear, is on this list. Two years after *PropOrNot* announced itself, a variant followed. NewsGuard purports to do what its name implies: It assigns itself the task of identifying misinformation, disinformation, and "fake news" inspired by "the Kremlin." For four dollars and ninety-five cents a month, NewsGuard advises subscribers—public institutions, libraries, universities, individuals—of offending publications. Once again, *Consortium News* is among the publications accused of purveying false information—information that is, with extensive evidence, perfectly accurate. I know this: I wrote some of the pieces with which NewsGuard took issue.

In the spring of 2023, we learned of another such group. Hamilton 68 began operating at roughly the same time NewsGuard started soliciting subscribers. Its self-assigned brief was, once again, to identify "disinformation" and "fake news" it purported to demonstrate was Russian-inspired. This was a highly sophisticated undertaking. Hamilton 68 employed advanced data analysis, or so it claimed, and presented itself as a computerized service—a "dashboard"—intended for use by journalists and scholars. The number of media that cited Hamilton 68 as a credible source is not short of extraordinary. These included *The New York Times*, *The Washington Post*, the Public Broadcasting System, and all the major networks. None ever advised readers or viewers of who founded and ran Hamilton 68: senior Democratic Party operatives and Clinton campaign officials, as well as, per usual by this time, officials from the CIA, the FBI, and the Homeland Security Department.

*PropOrNot*, which appears to be inactive as I write these concluding pages, does not identify those who founded and operate the site, leaving them to preside as hooded inquisitors. NewsGuard is more forthright as to its identity. It "partners" with the State Department and the Pentagon. Its advisory board includes Michael Hayden, a retired general and formerly director of the CIA and the NSA, Tom Ridge, the first secretary of Homeland Security, and Anders Rasmussen, a former secretary-general of NATO. In our time, *PropOrNot*, NewsGuard, Hamilton 68, and other such organizations, of which there appear to be numerous, pass as disinterested arbiters of what is true and false. These are among the pillars of the disinformation industry, as we come to call it—a private-public collaboration the objective of which is to suppress dissent. In their incessant invocations of Russophobia, they are the *Red Channels* of our time, and the comparison is useful for the historical context it lends our moment. They can be read as symptomatic of the many post-Russiagate excesses that have come to plague our press and our public space altogether.

A regime of censorship, very often urged on by journalists themselves, took shape as I was composing this final chapter. As in the case of Hamilton 68, much of this work is computerized by way of the algorithms through which digital media are managed. Publications or individual writers can be buried—difficult or impossible to find when readers search for them—or simply removed from a given platform. My own experience is instructive: As I was finishing these pages Twitter permanently censored my account, @thefloutist, offering no explanation other than to inform me I had "violated our community standards." It is a reasonable surmise that algorithms identified commentaries containing certain terms—"Ukraine," "Russia," "neo-Nazi," or "Syria" might be among these—and censors who read these columns found them objectionable. This is called "content moderation."

The circumstance I describe is dynamic. I am not aware of anyone who knows how far digital media will carry this new censorship. Marc Andreessen, the founder of Netscape, the web services company, and an influential figure in Silicon Valley, suggests digital media are on the way to a totalized system of information control. In the spring of 2022 Andreessen sent out this note via Twitter:

> I predict essentially identical censorship/deplatforming policies across all layers of the internet stack. Client-side & server-side ISPs, cloud platforms, CDNs, payment networks, client OSs, browsers, email clients. With only rare exceptions. The pressure is intense.

In effect, Andreessen describes the final phase of a long effort to bring the internet under control. We can now safely surmise that its original promise, to democratize the flow of information and to serve as a public forum unmediated by either official power or ideologically driven publications beholden to official power, was viewed by these same interests as a threat from the internet's earliest days. Censorship, the disinformation industry, official intervention into digital platforms, algorithmic formulae used to identify all who deviate from the orthodoxies: These are the tools by which the internet is not so gradually being converted into an instrument of social control.

Considerable damage has already been done to our public discourse. We now have earnest debates as to the First Amendment's validity, those defending it dismissed as retrograde purists. Journalists at *The New York Times*, *The Washington Post*, most of the dailies that follow their lead, the wires, and the broadcasters stand among those urging ever more rigorous censorship of dissident or alternative opinion or, very often, open debate of questions of pressing public concern. Congress coerces social media platforms to suppress versions of events that do not conform to approved orthodoxies. The extent of these official interventions became clear in late 2022, when Elon Musk, Twitter's new owner, began releasing "The Twitter Files," immense volumes of internal email in which Twitter employees took orders from law-enforcement officials. This was almost certainly the fate of my Twitter account. Lining up the chronology as best I can, @thefloutist was permanently blocked in mid-2022 because it was on one of the lists the FBI routinely gave Twitter when it ordered *en masse* cancellations.

Threatened with legislation that would break up their monopolies, these platforms cooperate without discernible compunction. Facebook, YouTube, Reddit and other companies—whether Twitter will remain on this list is not at writing clear—now have former intelligence officials and military officers on their staffs to identify "harmful" content to be removed. This is the intense pressure of which Andreessen wrote. It is official censorship at one remove—unlawful state censorship privatized. The latest turn in this regression is the most disturbing: We are now seeing efforts in the U.S.—and in Europe—to codify censorship practices into law. At writing, there is legislation pending on Capitol Hill that will, if passed, punish with prison terms or fines those who use private networks, called VPNs, to read material published on blacklisted websites. All this is done in the name of combating "disinformation"—as defined by those with long records of disseminating disinformation, records that are beyond dispute.

The control the national security state exerts over digital platforms is of a piece with the extensive compromises the traditional press and broadcasters have made since 2001. I do not see that we can avoid a disturbing conclusion: We are now faced with a more or less seamless integration of corporate media with various agencies and appendages of government. An information monoculture, and by easy extension a form of thought control, presses itself upon us. We do not have a plausible claim to be shocked by this circumstance if we bear history in mind.

S OME YEARS AGO, as the decline of American media became evident even among those not in the profession, friends and acquaintances began to ask two questions. Do journalists believe what they report and write? Or do they know what they tell us is misleading or false but mislead or lie so as to keep their jobs? I had no ready reply to these queries, but I welcomed them as measures of a healthy loss of faith, another "dis-illusioning." They suggested a reading and viewing public that was more aware, more alert to the crisis in our media, as the public was when Henry Luce financed the Hutchins Commission.

To attempt a reply to these inquiries now, in journalism today we have a remarkably prevalent case of Sartre's *mauvaise foi*. Bad faith, in terms I hope are not too simplified, comes down to pretending to be someone or something other than oneself. It means surrendering authenticity, that essential value in Sartre's thinking. In bad faith one enacts a role to meet the expectations of others as one imagines them to be. Sartre's famous example is the café waiter whose every move-ment—"a little too precise, a little too rapid"—is an artificial display of what he thinks patrons expect a café waiter to be. In philosophic terms, it is a question of "being-for-others" as against "being-for-it-self." A former journalist made the point very simply in the comment thread appended to one of my columns. "I was like most of the jour-nalists I knew over the decades I spent off-and-on in the business. I was a faker."

This is the American journalist as he or she has come to be, a journalist-for-others. The less he genuinely serves as a journalist—a journalist-for-itself—the more he must hold to the accepted image of the journalist. He is "the man without a shadow," as Jung put it in another context. Having become another of society's "de-indi-vidualized persons"—Jung again—the journalist role-plays now, in psychotherapeutic terms. Newspapers, in the same way, are at bottom reënactments of newspapers.

To inquiring friends, I now say journalists are not liars, not pre-cisely. "A man does not lie about what he is ignorant of," Sartre wrote in *Being and Nothingness*, "he does not lie when he spreads an error of which he is a dupe." It is our perfect term for the unmoored journalist of our time. We come again to the turning of Descartes upside down. "I think, therefore I am" becomes "I am, therefore I think." This is what I mean: *I am a* Washington Post *reporter, and these, therefore, are my thoughts and this my understanding of the world I report upon.*

Self-deception of the kind I describe is one of two forces sustaining the malpractice of journalism on the newsroom floor. It would be difficult to overstate its power. Breathe fetid air long enough and you have no notion of a spring breeze. I have never met a journalist in the condition of bad faith capable of recognizing what he has done to himself in the course of his professional life—his alienation, the artifice of which he and his work are made. Self-illusioning is a totality in the consciousness.

The second such force is intimately related to the first and in its practical aspect is still more compelling. I refer here to what Upton Sinclair called, a century ago, "the brass check." We must now consider money. Is there any self-deception under the sun that money cannot ask for and usually receive?

Sinclair considered *The Brass Check* one of the two most important books he ever wrote, the other being *The Jungle*. He self-published it in 1919 and left it un-copyrighted with the thought that it should be freely available. It is a vigorous, four hundred forty-five-page indictment of the American press in all its disfigurement. It is not well-written: The prose is graceless, frequently shrill, and dense with dated references. But it is virtuously relentless. It gives us historic ballast with which to understand that the crisis in American journalism today is a story with a long history. For all its peculiarities, the book is especially pertinent to our time. Robert McChesney, the noted media critic, brought out a new edition at the University of Illinois Press in 2003.

Sinclair was a curious man. He was raised in comfortable circumstances in New York and settled in Pasadena, but there was much of the prairie populist in his contempt for American capitalism. *The Brass Check* is a condemnation of the power of capital to corrupt the press, and Sinclair judged it to corrupt absolutely. "Not hyperbolically and contemptuously, but literally and with scientific precision," he wrote contemptuously, "we define journalism in America as the business and practice of presenting the news of the day in the interest of economic privilege."

It is the story of the brass check that drew me back to Sinclair's book. He heard it while a college student in New York at the turn of the twentieth century. Brass checks seem to have been part of the prostitution scene then. A client arrived at his favored bordello and paid the madam for an evening's pleasure. In return he received a chit in the form of a brass check, and when the woman of his choice took him upstairs, he handed her the chit. At evening's end the prostitute returned the brass check to the madam. The john went home satisfied (presumably), the lady of the night was fairly paid (presumably), and the proprietor kept control of the money.

The story made a lasting impression on the young Sinclair. "There is more than one kind of parasite feeding on human weakness, there is more than one kind of prostitution which may be symbolized by the BRASS CHECK," he recalled in the book he published two decades later. "The Brass Check is found in your pay envelope every week— you who write and print and distribute our newspapers and magazines. The Brass Check is the price of your shame—you who take the fair body of truth and sell it in the market-place, who betray the virgin hopes of mankind into the loathsome brothel of big business."

That is Sinclair—seething, tipping not infrequently into the purplish prose of outrage. But he makes a strong if histrionic case for his outrage. He confirms a judgment I have earlier suggested. There is vastly more at stake in the misconduct of American journalists today than there was in Sinclair's time. America has since made itself a global power. It is all the more remarkable to ponder the extent to which the information war that weighs decisively on so many momentous global events is sustained by editors and correspondents whose primary concerns are their everyday material desires—houses, cars, evenings out, holidays. This is what I saw again and again during my years in the mainstream press. This, a problem of proportion, is hard to reconcile, as it was more parochially so in Sinclair's day, but it is still the problem as he identified it.

Sinclair falls off the deep end as he concludes *The Brass Check*. "Now, surely, this mystery is a mystery no longer!" he exclaims. "Now we know what the seer of Patmos was foreseeing—Capitalist Journalism! And when I call upon you, class-conscious workers of hand and brain, to organize and destroy this mother of all iniquities, I do not have to depart from the language of the ancient scriptures." He goes on to quote from Ezekiel.

*The Brass Check* ends with just such a departure, thankfully. In a section subheaded "A Practical Program," Sinclair lays out a way forward from the mother of iniquities he has finished parsing. "I propose that we shall found and endow a weekly publication of truth-telling to be known as 'The National News,'" he writes. Here is Sinclair on the kind of paper he thought America needed:

> It will not be a journal of opinion, but a record of events pure and simple. It will be published on ordinary news-print paper, and in the cheapest possible form. It will have one purpose and one purpose only, to give the American people once every week the truth about the world's events. It will be strictly and absolutely nonpartisan, and never the propaganda organ of any cause. It will watch the country, and see where lies are being circulated and truth suppressed; its job will be to nail the lies, and bring the truth to the light of day.

This is neither more nor less than an invocation of the ideal of objectivity considered earlier—never attainable, ever to be striven for. "The National News" would carry no advertising, so protecting itself against the coercions of corporate interests. This would require a subsidy so as to keep the price down—a subsidy "large enough to make success certain." Sinclair defines success as precisely as he does all else: "I believe that a sufficient number of Americans are awake to the dishonesty of our press to build up for such a paper a circulation of a million inside a year."

No newspaper called "The National News" ever came to be. But we err to conclude Sinclair's project died before it could be born. I have a good idea Cedric Belfrage and Jim Aronson read *The Brass Check*, given the book's excellent sales and enduring reputation. But no matter. When they founded the *National Guardian* in 1948, they tore a page straight from Sinclair's book. The project was journalism untainted by power or money and supported by readers who valued the undertaking.

I wish I had read *The Brass Check* before I went to work in that memoried loft on West Seventeenth Street. It was at the *Guardian* that I first encountered the inverse relationship that so often obtains between power and money on one hand, and uncompromised, plain-spoken journalism on the other. When I consider how American journalists can find their way out of the crisis to which they have brought the profession, my thoughts arise from those ninety-a-week years in my mid-twenties. I can see this now as I could not for a long time after those days came to an end and as my path led elsewhere.

I HAVE NEVER CARED for the term "alternative media." There are only media, in my view. They are of greater or lesser quality, integrity, and reliability; they have greater or fewer resources at their disposal and greater or lesser reach. Our media have more or less power, one to the next, and a larger or smaller place in public discourse. But "alternative," a term that seems to have arisen among other-than-mainstream media themselves, is a great disservice. It places the alternative in a diminished position next to standard-setting superiors, so confirming them as perennially in opposition to a prior version of events. This is no longer remotely the case, if ever it was. The best so-called alternative media are now emphatically *for*—for discernible truths, for objective accounts of events that stand on their own two feet—accounts, indeed, that often enough have not appeared elsewhere.

"Independent media" is the better and accepted term now—independent of corporate owners and advertisers, of political and institutional power, of prevailing orthodoxies. Although it is not much used, I also favor "nonaligned media." Robert Parry, a refugee from the mainstream when he founded *Consortium News* in 1995, put this point as well as anyone ever has when, twenty years later, he accepted the Neiman Foundation's I. F. Stone Medal for Journalistic Independence. "To me the core responsibility of a journalist is to have an open mind toward information, to have no agenda, to have no preferred outcome," he said on that occasion. He then added the summation I quoted earlier: "In other words, I don't care what the truth is. I just care what the truth is."

Apart from the sheer dignity of these words, implicit in them is the thought that the place of independent media has fundamentally changed in the last decade or so. The mainstream's turn toward agenda-driven journalism during the Trump and Russiagate years, so well described by Jim Rutenberg and the others I have cited, was decisive, in my view. Corporate media retain immense influence and continue to enjoy large and loyal followings—there is no suggesting otherwise. But for an ever-growing number of readers and viewers, these media's subservience to the national security state is greatly more obvious. All mainstream journalism is "embedded journalism" now, for the battlefield is everywhere. This places burdens on independent publications far outsized to their means. Let us not allow this circumstance to distract us. It is a matter of independent, nonaligned journalists understanding the responsibilities that fall to them now and then embracing these with alacrity.

Mainstream journalists do not often produce the first draft of history, as the creaky adage has it, however much they may or may not have done so in the past. Journalism in our time and by the evidence in many others is the first draft of the accounting of things power prefers so as to keep balanced, factual accounts of events, those bearing on the conduct of empire at home and abroad, out of history books. Journalists outside the mainstream are thus the historian's true friends and bear the first-draft duty the historian imposes. The Russiagate affair is a case in point. While the mainstream piled proven fallacies and far-fetched conspiracies one atop another, such mis- and disinformation is unlikely to survive a good historian's scrutiny given the work independent journalists have written into the record. The task is to force the great unsayable into what is said. This is done whenever journalists speak the language that is not spoken, the language wherein truth resides. It is the task of a press that is truly responsible.

The appetite for this kind of work among readers and viewers is impossible to miss at this point. This, too, confers a responsibility on independent journalists. Readers come to recognize what I have argued severally in my columns: We can no longer read *The Times*, and by extension the rest of the corporate press, to learn of events, to know what happened. We read *The Times* to know what we are supposed to think happened. Then we go in search of accurate accounts of what happened. Do not take this as an indulgence of cynical wit. The observation arises out of numerous cases wherein this unfortunate reality has proven so.

I am not alone in advocating a top-to-bottom renovation of the craft—meaning a recovery of journalism as an autonomous institution, a pole of power, a Fourth Estate, antiquated as this term may seem. This transformation is to be accomplished over a long period of time, not by grand convocations or scholarly symposia but in the sheer doing of it. It would be foolish to count on established media to drive this process. They may find their way back from the swamp of subjectivity, or return to their senses on the censorship question, or recover from their altogether curious swoon into "wokery" and "identity politics" in their newsrooms. But with the history I have reviewed as our guide, there is simply no ground to expect mainstream media to reclaim the independence they long ago surrendered to the national security state—not under present circumstances. I detect only faint signs of debate among these media on this question, the most decisive they face, for they refuse, as they did during and after the Cold War, to recognize the errors, the dysfunction.

Every journalist now practicing faces a choice none was ever trained to confront. "If journalism is anything," John Pilger said in a television appearance as I wrote this chapter, "you are an agent of people, not power." This is the choice I mean. It has always been there, but in our time it has become too evident and stark to avoid. It is by way of independent media that journalists can make this choice. There are only media, but the independent among them are destined now to matter ever more.

MY THINKING ABOUT THIS DESTINY draws from an unlikely source and is informed, I must mention, by the peculiarities of my professional path. Some readers may remember Jerzy Grotowski, the Polish theater director and theorist prominent in the nineteen sixties. *Towards a Poor Theater*, published in 1968, proved influential well beyond theatrical circles. I read it while still at university, but it was decades before I saw any connection between Grotowski's thinking and the profession I chose. From his "poor theater" I derive "a poor journalism." Cedric Belfrage and Jim Aronson could not have described what they were doing in these terms. But they advocated precisely this two decades before Grotowski suggested their endeavor might have a name. My *Guardian* years were my first experience living a poor journalism.

Grotowski's project began with a radical stripping away. He saw modern theater as encrusted with convention, artifice, and "plastic elements"—costumes, makeup, artful lighting, elaborate stage sets. This was distracting junk at the expense of integrity, in Grotowski's estimation. Modern theater was "rich theater"—mere spectacle, overweighted with accoutrements. With naturalism the aesthetic, the proscenium was a confinement for actors and audience alike: There were different realities on either side of it. Performers were alienated not just from the house but, more poignantly, from their own thoughts, emotions, and bodies. Grotowski often wrote of "life-masks," the internalized conventions actors traditionally work within. To me, he was concerned with the difference between the presented self, the performing self, the self of bad faith, and against these the genuine self, "the face"—I revert to Jung here—"we never show the world because we cover it with the *persona*, the mask of the actor." This is the Jungian shadow as I have used this term.

From Grotowski:

> If we strip ourselves and touch an extraordinarily intimate layer, the life-mask cracks and falls away.

And:

> This defiance of taboo... provides the shock which rips off the mask.

And:

> In this struggle with one's own truth, this effort to peel away the life-mask, with its full-fleshed perceptivity, has always seemed to me a place of provocation.

To transcend the roles imposed by convention, to destroy distance in favor of closeness and the most complete authenticity humans can achieve: This is poor theater.

The concept arose from the simplest of questions. Grotowski asked: What is theater? When all that is not essential is taken away, what remains? He replied that when rich theater's furnishings and clutter are removed, it transforms the performer-audience relationship: They enter the rawest kind of contact possible. Grotowski trained his actors very rigorously to connect, above all and as honestly as possible, with themselves; then could they connect most directly and effectively with audiences.

I borrowed and bent Grotowski's question long ago when I devised my irreducible definition of journalism: Before it is anything else, it is at bottom seeing and saying, nothing more. Scrape away the superfluous and all the barnacles of convention and you have observation, reporting, and writing or speaking or filming. All the accreted encumbrances—the deference to official authority, the narrow limits defining "acceptable" sources and perspectives, the dense language of bureaucrats, above all the pretense to Lippmannite professionalism and membership in social and administrative elites—are eligible for removal. Much of this, or maybe most or all of it, derives one way or another from the unhealthy relations with power I have dwelled upon in these chapters. To political, corporate, and financial power I can now add bureaucratic power, the power of editorial hierarchies, the power of embedded ethical corruptions—altogether the inertia and lethargy draped over the profession. The journalist as seer and sayer discards all this. The corrupting of accuracy and honesty in exchange for access is worse now than one could have imagined even a few years ago. So is the self-censorship transmitted throughout the system. A poor journalism makes it possible to withdraw all offers to bargain integrity for access or acceptance on terms other than the journalist's own. This would mark a consequential turn in itself: It would be one step on for journalists to shed the burden of self-censorship, for the invisible mechanisms that enforce it will lose their leverage.

As I may by now have made plain, I am especially sensitive to the power of language as it is used in the cause either of clarity and understanding or of obfuscation and ignorance. To assume the language of institutions and the language of sources and those covered—"global leadership," "collateral damage," "regime change," "the intelligence community," "the rules-based order," and so on through the bureaucratic lexicon—is to work in obscuring euphemisms, if not falsifications. It is the single most effective device forcing journalists into the state of alienation from the self that is common among them. Orwell described how the language of ideologues and obscurantist mandarins devastates our ability to think clearly—precisely its purpose—in "Politics and the English Language." Since he published his essay in

*Horizon* in April 1946, the problem as we have it is seven decades' worth of worse.

This use of language has disarmed language itself, depriving it of its assertive power such that speech or writing outside the orthodoxy can be dismissed as a site of serious discourse. Language is rendered impotent as a medium of creative thought or as a prompt to new, imaginative action. The task of independent journalists, then, is restorative. It is to take language back, to renew its life, to wrest it from the deadening influence of institutions, bureaucracies, and corporate media—these having deformed language into an instrument for the enforcement of conformity.

So does the journalism I write of hold clear language as its instrument—unadorned, written and spoken plainly, colloquial in the best sense of this term but perfectly capable of subtlety and complexity. It is the language of neither exceptionalism nor of empire. It is the language of history, not myth. This language understands journalism as a subset of humanism, not American nationalism—"patriotism," as we are urged to call it. It is the language necessary to confront power rather than accommodate it. It is language that presumes the utility of intelligence and critical thought. It is meant for the posing of many worthy questions. It is unreservedly dedicated to enlarging the sayable in hostile response to the great American unsayable. By way of this language a more vibrant, fulfilling national discourse awaits us.

I describe altogether a cleansing, a rejuvenation in the literal meaning of this term—an embrace of what we can think of as youthful vigor. Rich journalism is the journalism of Lippmann, we can now understand. It relies on distances between journalists and readers and, the primal problem, between journalists wearing the life-masks of the Lippmannite profession and their authentic selves—in practice, between what they think they have to write or say apart from what they know. These distances—journalists from readers or viewers, journalists from themselves—are now fixed in the culture of the craft. Poor journalism, as I mean this term, would shrink these distances and reduce the attendant alienation. It would dismantle the proscenium, we can say, while making the journalist whole, integrated, not a stranger to his shadow or a performer in a role. Grotowski's retraining of actors was in large measure a psychological question: This is evident in everything he had to say about his poor theater. It is the same in journalism. My experience and all I have seen in the profession confirms me in this conviction. This is why I dwell in these pages on the psychological condition of the journalist in our time.

I describe an ideal, and I have already shared my thought as to the proximity of ideals. A poor journalism means a journalism more authentic than any we have heretofore known but rarely. This may seem a hopelessly angelic idea of what can be done to remedy our media culture's dysfunctions. Is this not so for many fundamental reforms, notably those urgently needed? Do they not, at the outset, appear too distant ever to be achieved? We must recognize what our moment asks of us. We do not begin with an assessment of what is possible—nothing interesting or of genuine use ever comes of this. We begin with what is necessary and then proceed to the hard work of making the necessary possible. Any journalist holding this book can think of it this way: To the extent this project seems beyond reach is precisely the extent to which it needs to get done. The magnitude of the task does not excuse us from undertaking it.

SOME YEARS AGO THE OVERSEAS PRESS CLUB, a long-moribund but lately revived institution in New York, gave one of its annual prizes to Amy Goodman, the host of *Democracy Now!* Goodman's reputation has since declined, regrettably, but she did well that evening. The award recognized the broadcast's coverage, over the course of the previous year, of a foreign story I can no longer recall. There were several hundred correspondents and editors in attendance, and Tom Brokaw, the network news presenter and social grandee, was master of ceremonies. Goodman took the podium, refused the prize, and began a vigorous critique of corporate media's abysmal coverage of foreign affairs during the year then passed, delivered in the direct manner for which she was then known. Brokaw instantly intervened: "No, no, no ... this is not the time...." Not until many of us stood and shouted him down was Goodman able to finish. It is a pity that Goodman and her program no longer hold to this kind of integrity and independence.

There is a truth in that evening's unseemly display. Journalists have to get poor in the common meaning of the term if the profession is to recover itself. I do not propose monastic vows or penury. I do not refer to reporters and editors paid ordinary salaries for, the best of them, honorable work. I begin with the upper ranks—the Brokaws and the other network stars, those "upper echelons" at *The Times* and the other major dailies. As Brokaw's outburst made plain, these people are too invested in the elites they are supposed to cover but instead desire to join. Whatever they may have been as they came up in the craft, too much money and aggrandizement have ruined them.

I navigated the mainstream for decades and know the power of the brass check well enough. During my *Daily News* days, a crusty sports editor nearing retirement told me that until a few years previously the Bureau of Labor Statistics classified reporters as blue-collar workers. Let us recall our Mencken in this connection. "A good reporter used to make as much as a bartender or a police sergeant," he wrote with evident investment in the matter. "He now makes as much as a doctor or lawyer, and probably a good deal more…. He has got a secure lodgment in a definite stratum." I mean to suggest, as Mencken did, that something was lost as journalists began to professionalize a century or so ago—something lost and worthy of restoration. Let us define this something, as Mencken would and as Upton Sinclair would, as the journalist's freedom to do unsullied work—"with no strings tied to him," as Mencken put it in his recollections.

In a single word, journalists must become and remain unincorporated if they are to amount to more than the clerks of the governing class, and this I mean in all senses of the term. Disenfranchised will also do. I. F. Stone, a man of great stature and unassuming means, used to say journalists are properly outsiders. This, too, serves the thought. The unique place they should occupy, in society but not altogether of it, must be observed—honored, even. This requires a distance from power that allows them to remain faithful to themselves and their ethics. Money does not serve this purpose; modest living does—comfortable-enough, rent-paying, family-raising, modest living. Have we become so grand that this is a strange idea? It is the precondition of authentic disinterest and immunity from intimidation. The adversarial position in the face of power and a reconnection with readers and viewers require this—a kind of disinvestment. Let all aspiration and imagination soar, but the work is the reward, not places at high table.

Can this transformation of the journalist's identity be accomplished within the confines of our most powerful media institutions?

My profound doubts should by now be plain. The current ownership structure of American media appears to make this impossible. In effect, they rely on the "dis-integration" of their editors, reporters, and correspondents to publish and broadcast as they do. But let us count it an outstanding question, even if it is theoretically so as things now stand. If corporate media are to find their way out of their current malaise, I am certain it will be in large part because independent media have forced them, by the example of their best work, to do so.

When I first transliterated a poor, authentic theater into a poor, authentic journalism, it was difficult to say how long it would take for any such remaking of the craft to be realized, or if ever it would be. Who would choose such a path? It was long and remains so, surely. Each generation produces but a few true, genuinely committed journalists who understand what they do as nearer to a calling than merely a job. I cannot postulate a mass repudiation of the brass check, after all. Belfrage and Aronson's very fine idea and my years at the paper they founded seemed long ago—a time, like all times past, beyond retrieval.

But the riches to be reaped by way of a poor journalism grow more evident now. Independent, nonaligned journalism as we have it and to my surprise, is poor journalism made flesh, and its power accumulates as we speak. In this it would be hard to overstate the importance of the new and elaborating internet technologies available to independent practitioners. Belfrage and Aronson, I. F. Stone, Seymour Hersh, Robert Scheer, John Pilger, and other such figures: While they began their professional years in a pre-digital time and with fewer publishing alternatives, they were lighters of the way. There are now nearly countless dailies and weeklies coming out just as traditional publications do. When Bob Parry started *Consortium News* in 1995, it was among the first of these to appear, and Bob understood what poor journalism meant without ever hearing the term. One-person operations—Glenn Greenwald, John Pilger, Caitlin Johnstone, Chris Hedges, Eva Bartlett, the excellent Jonathan Cook, numerous others—publish and raise sustaining subscriptions via Medium, Substack, or similar platforms developed for writers. There are sui generis enterprises such as the previously mentioned *Grayzone*, an investigative website whose name calls to mind a poem by Taduesz Różewich, the Polish modernist:

> my gray zone
> is starting to include poetry
>
> here white is not absolute white
> black is not absolute black
> the edges of these non-colors
> adjoin

If this is the inspiration of Max Blumenthal, *The Grayzone*'s founder and editor, his thought is perfectly to the point: Let the work of independents be as elegant as anything else out there, let it be colorblind—nonaligned in my terminology.

A cacophonous choir of many voices and as many political stripes is audible all around us now. The worst of it is the bad work of untrained amateurs and strolling players, but this is nothing new in journalism, mainstream or otherwise. The best is disciplined, professionally executed journalism whose only agenda is fidelity to the facts and evidence unearthed in the course of reporting. This is more important now than it was even during the Cold War decades, in my view, given the national security state's aggressive disinformation campaigns in the post-2001 period, and now our disinformation industry.

Let us consider the case of the U.N.'s Organization for the Prohibition of Chemical Weapons. In 2019 and 2020, conclusive evidence emerged that the OPCW, coerced by Washington, suppressed its inspectors' findings that a chemical weapons attack staged in 2018 and blamed on the Assad government in Damascus was another false-flag operation intended to draw the US directly into the Syrian conflict. Nothing of this corruption, momentous as it is, has ever been reported in the corporate press. Various independent media, including Amy Goodman's *Democracy Now!,* have also ignored abundant evidence of falsification revealed by OPCW whistleblowers. It was the independent Aaron Maté who exposed Washington's intimidation of the OPCW. While *The New York Times* and the rest of the mainstream press continue to leave this scandal unreported, Maté wrote it into the record—where, next to it, he also wrote in corporate media's silence. As Maté's experience suggests, mainstream media are at this point at war with those producing sound journalism independently. Their intent is plain: It is to reassert their long-established but now challenged monopoly over accepted narratives.

Technologies are not value-neutral. They are not empty of content other than what is put into them. Implicit in any technology is an affirmation of the political economy and material circumstances that produced it. This is another of Jacques Ellul's lessons. The technologies now available to independent journalists are corporate products. They are vital to independent practitioners as means of delivery, but, as we learn by the day now, access to them can be withdrawn at any time. This is a contradiction we must recognize and consider. As we do, we are led to ask: Can the promise of independent journalism be extinguished by way of a totalized system of censorship such as Marc Andreessen described in that disturbing note he sent out in April 2022?

I see no chance of this, dangerous as highly coordinated efforts to suppress dissent have become. The question, indeed, seems to miss what is more fundamentally at issue and of worth in independent media. Clever uses of new technologies have nothing to do with this. It is the commitment of independent journalists such as Jonathan Cook that, for the time being, matters most. These are, and I would say without exception, professionals who understand that independent publications make it possible to refuse to surrender their shadows to the requisite "dis-integration" and alienation. It is in this way I write of these publications as refuges. They are sites of integration, and so of integrity. "If the individual is not truly regenerated in spirit, society cannot be either," Jung wrote in *The Undiscovered Self*, "for society is the sum total of individuals in need of redemption." Fromm, a Freudian, made the same point in his *Escape from Freedom*. If we substitute "journalism" for "society" in this passage, the point will be plain. It is rededication to integrity that determines the value of what any journalist conveys by way of any technology. This is what is truly new in the current renaissance of independent journalism. If I can call what it stands for an ideal, it is not an ideal censors have any hope of suppressing.

Jerzy Grotowski's book achieved note beyond the theater because, intentionally or otherwise, it reflected the spirit of its time. It appeared amid a marked desire in the West to break out of the confinements and encrustations of official culture and its attendant politics. The project, if I do not put this too simply, was for humanity to connect with itself in some transcendent, historically new way—to crack all its life-masks. I read something of this into the unspoken ideals of independent journalists. They seek, the best of them, to dispose of the barriers behind which mainstream practitioners hide from readers and from themselves, and in this they seem to express some larger restlessness abroad among us—some desire for a new consciousness of new twenty-first century realities and thereby of ourselves. Proximity to readers is independent journalism's reply to Lippmannite distance. In Deweyesque fashion, passive spectators become active participants in the conveyance of information and perspectives. There is responsiveness, accessibility, an engagement that flows in both directions. Social media and comment threads appended to published work do much to make this possible.

I HAVE WRITTEN of the long arc of the national security state's efforts to incorporate American newspapers and broadcasters into the ranks of its allied institutions, and of these media's willingness to assume this place. But the resulting crisis does not belong only to those who actively made it, or those who passively participated in it as journalists. If American media have made a mess of themselves over the course of many years, as I have contended in these pages, it is also ours—we who have averted our eyes or otherwise could not see it as it was made. So is the remedy ours, too.

It is not a pretty story, the one I have told, but it is ours to write new and good chapters in it. Our traditional media have spoken. What they are is plain. The reply is ours to make.

# Acknowledgements.

I HAVE NAMED but few of the colleagues, professional acquaintances, and friends who walk through this book, and they are too numerous to name now. I am grateful to have worked with or alongside all of them.

I wish to mention a few people especially deserving of my fond thanks across many years. Cara Marianna saw this book through its drafts and revisions with the greatest intelligence, care, and affection. This book would not be as you have it without her. My other readers, and my gratitude to all of them, were Peter Dimock of Tarrytown, New York, Paul Sillitoe of Withiel Florey, Somerset, Allen Baker of Ashland, Oregon, David Hendrickson of Colorado Springs, Kevin Fathi of Gadsden, Alabama, Muriel Davis of New York, and Eva-Maria Föllmer-Müller of Zurich. There is at last Augusto, my long-lost *companheiro*, whose generous assistance and friendship during my Lisbon days remains with me, and there is his sister, Anna, who knitted me *um barrete preto pescador* that still warms my ears on winter walks. *Um abraço* across the decades.

*—Norfolk, Conn.,*
*Lago de Chapala, Jalisco.*
*Winter 2020–Spring 2023.*